THE NAVY FROM WOOD TO STEEL

⚓

THE WATTS HISTORIES OF
THE UNITED STATES NAVY

⚓

THE NAVY
FROM
WOOD TO STEEL

1860–1890

⚓

Daniel J. Carrison,

CAPTAIN, U. S. N.

FRANKLIN WATTS, INC.
575 Lexington Avenue, New York 22

FIRST PRINTING
Copyright © 1965 by Franklin Watts, Inc.
Library of Congress Catalog Card Number: 65-11939
Printed in the United States of America

Contents

⚓

Author's Foreword

⚓

DURING THE PERIOD 1860 to 1890, the United States Navy rose from lethargic doldrums to become the largest navy in the world. Then, having won international recognition and acclaim, it sank again into oblivion. The Navy's phenomenal growth occurred in the first five years of this period—the deadly years of 1860–65, when bloody Civil War tore the Union apart. This was a fascinating era in naval history, filled with colorful characters and deeds of valor. It was a time when relatively obscure men became famous overnight, and were toasted across the country. The names of Farragut, Porter, Foote, and DuPont became household words.

After the war, and until the close of the century, a small band of dedicated naval officers carried on through years of austere funding and isolationist thinking. In the 1880's, when several South American nations had navies better than ours, an intellectual renaissance and an awareness of growing destiny stirred the country to look once more to the sea. Under the guidance of a farseeing Congress, the United States rebuilt maritime yards and embarked on a ship construction program that made the United States Navy a new force for peace and security in the community of nations.

—Daniel J. Carrison,
Captain, U.S.N.

ONE

⚓

Union Sea Power

Many books have been written about the Civil War but most of them fail to tell in detail the important work accomplished by the Union navy. Actually, sea power played an immense and decisive role in that war, although its influence was overshadowed by the more glamorous achievements of land armies.

The North had a one-sided advantage at sea and put it to good use. The power of the Union navy slowly demoralized the South and wore down the Confederacy's will to resist. Union blockade squadrons choked off foreign trade and threw the agricultural South upon its own meager industrial resources.

Leaders of the Confederacy looked in vain to Europe for naval assistance, hoping that "King Cotton" would bring England and France to their rescue. Unfortunately for the South this assistance never materialized. In 1861 European warehouses were filled with cotton produced by the bumper crop of 1860. Textile mills in England and France made use of this inventory through the first years of the war, and thus there was no fear of a cotton shortage. Consequently, the South was left to fight an opponent which hopelessly outnumbered it at sea.

Wars are usually won by armies; however, history shows that the combination of land and sea power has generally defeated land power alone. The influence of sea power is slow to take effect and it is more important in a long war of attrition than in a short war. Sea power is more than mere naval strength. While naval strength is necessary, sea power is the sum total of weapons, industrial capacity, and geographical circumstances which enable a nation to control the seas in wartime. Shipyards, heavy industry, ports, bases, a seafaring people, a commercial maritime fleet—all of these are important elements of sea power.

The North had an advantage over the South in almost every one of these elements. In the first place, the North had a navy and the South had none. Most of the country's industrial capacity, shipyards, maritime shipping fleet, and merchant seamen were north of the Mason-Dixon Line. There was not a single plant in the South capable of building a marine engine. The Confederacy approximated the North only in the number of seaports and in the size of its commercial river fleet.

On paper, the North's advantage looked greater than it actually was. The sea arm of the Union was limp. In 1861 Secretary of the Navy Gideon Welles had ninety ships in his navy, but fifty of them were obsolete. In the years of strict economy before the war, the United States was slow to change from sail to steam, from side-wheel paddles to screw propellers, and from smoothbore guns to rifled cannons. Many gunboats lay rotting in navy yards and some of the thirty-eight-ship steamer fleet were so run down that their engines would not operate.

The Union navy's five new frigates—*Merrimac, Colorado, Roanoke, Minnesota,* and *Wabash*—were the equal of any in the world. Measuring 269 feet in length and 51 feet in breadth, they carried forty-two 9-inch rifled cannons, one 11-inch rifle, four 100-pound rifles, and one 150-pound rifle. Unfortunately, they had been laid up out of commission as an economy measure before the war commenced. The active ships which bore the brunt of the early Civil War fighting included seven first-class screw sloops, eight smaller second-class screw sloops, and four side-wheelers. All but three of the warships capable of operating were cruising on foreign station—in the Mediterranean, off the African coast on antislavery patrol, or in the Western Pacific. When war began and President Lincoln declared the blockade of the Confederacy, only three propeller-driven ships, *Mohawk* and *Crusader* in New York and *Pawnee* in Washington, were available to enforce it. Altogether these ships mounted a total of only twenty-one guns.

[4]

Moreover, the Navy personnel situation caused justifiable concern. While the Army's West Point had produced young officers who made brilliant records in the Mexican War and in action on the Indian Frontier, few of the Navy's Annapolis graduates had risen above the rank of lieutenant when the Civil War started. Long years of peace and the unrealistic practice of promotion by seniority had clogged officer lists, and the best jobs in the Navy were filled with elderly veterans. Promotion by seniority meant that every officer who lived long enough and stayed out of trouble automatically went to the top of the list. Able and alert younger officers stagnated in subordinate positions. It was not unusual in the Navy of this period to find passed midshipmen in their thirties and lieutenants in their forties. The U.S. Navy officer corps was described as a "routine body of men without initiative" headed by "wornout men without brains." While this was somewhat harsh criticism, it was the opinion held at the time; however, as we shall see, there were some outstanding and daring leaders left.

Shortly after the firing on Fort Sumter there came agonizing moments when men of honor had to decide where their loyalties lay. About one-third of the Union navy's officers "went South" with their states to build the Confederate navy. Among them was Captain Raphael Semmes who became the most famed commerce raider of the Confederacy. There was also Matthew F. Maury, the oceanographer of world renown; Captain Franklin Buchanan, the commander of the Washington Navy Yard; and Commodore Josiah Tattnall, who had coined the phrase "blood is thicker than water" when he took American ships to the aid of the British during a Chinese uprising in 1859.

On the other hand, many prominent Southern officers remained loyal to the Union. Chief among these was David Glasgow Farragut, who was Tennessee-born and who had married a Southern girl. Admired in Navy circles for denouncing Virginia's secession and for giving up his home and property in Norfolk, Farragut was given responsible commands in the first year of the war. In 1861 Farragut was sixty, but his vitality belied his forty-nine years' naval service.

Three years later he was made a vice admiral. By an Act of Congress, he became the first U.S. naval officer to attain the rank of admiral.

The Navy Department itself was firmly led by "Uncle Gideon" Welles, who had been appointed Secretary of the Navy by President Lincoln as a political gesture to New England. Welles was chiefly known as a politician and editor of the Hartford *Times*. He knew very little about the navy, but he was a tireless worker and an excellent administrator. Secretary Welles was reticent and thoughtful, but he was a rock of strength in Lincoln's cabinet.

Welles relied heavily on his able assistant, Gustavus Fox. Also a New Englander, Fox was the exact opposite of Welles. He was gay and generous, loved to meet people, and despised being tied to a desk. "Gus" Fox was a small man, described as being "five feet nothing," who had served eighteen years as a naval officer. Disgusted with the U.S. Navy's slow promotion system, he had resigned to enter business in Massachusetts. Early in 1861 Lincoln offered Fox a ship in the Union navy and a volunteer officer's commission, but Fox's father-in-law, Postmaster General Montgomery Blair, advised him to take a position in the Navy Department if possible. Congress created the new post of Assistant Secretary of the Navy in July 1861 and Gus Fox became the first appointee. Fortunately the two top civilian directors of the Union navy got on perfectly together. Both were imaginative and daring, and neither hesitated to drop old ideas in favor of new and original schemes.

From the start of the war it was clearly evident that the navy's primary job would be to blockade the Confederate coast and operate on inland rivers. Welles and Fox immediately recognized the need for naval expansion and embarked on a course that increased the navy's blockading force from 3 ships to a total of 264 in a few months. The frigates of the *Minnesota* class were too large for close work in shallow coastal waters, and it was dangerous for them to venture into the tortuous river channels of the South. Smaller ships were needed. The two amateur naval strategists launched a buying spree to collect almost all craft that floated. They purchased whalers, yachts, tugs, ferryboats, and first-class steamers, and promptly converted them to warships by installing naval cannons. Next they turned to Yankee industrialists for new construction, and sent hurried recalls to ships then on foreign station.

Ship construction had its problems. The army drew heavily upon the machine shops and skilled workmen who were capable of heavy construction, but Secretary Welles cut enough red tape to get the job done. The first twenty-three ships constructed were the so-called "90-day" gunboats. These were shallow draft boats of five hundred tons which mounted one 11-inch pivot gun and four 23-pound howitzers. Once the gunboat program was underway, Welles contracted for the construction of sloops of war suitable for ocean cruising and fast enough to chase down Southern blockade-runners.

Union naval authorities soon found that screw-propeller steamers were hopelessly inefficient in the narrow, winding channels of the South. Side-wheelers and double-enders of extreme maneuverability could outperform screw-ships in restricted waters. However, the side-wheelers were more vulnerable under fire, so the department shifted its emphasis to double-enders for river warfare. "Double-enders" were arranged like ferries, with rudders and propellers at each end and engines which could go ahead or back with equal ability.

The Federal navy expanded steadily in spite of the chaos of early reverses, defection of personnel, and loss of navy yards in the South. This trial period was a true test of a civilian secretary whose main task was to handle the business end of a military service. "Uncle Gideon" survived his trial with flying colors. He felt his way slowly at first and then assumed extraordinary emergency powers. Significantly, there was not a single instance of scandal in his department during the entire course of the war.

With the ship-procurement program well started, Welles turned his attention to personnel. He had to replace the officers of the U.S. Navy who had "gone South" and find new officers for his expanding force. At his request, Congress passed legislation which discarded the seniority promotion system for officers and created the rank of admiral. Secretary Welles gradually retired senior officers at the age of sixty-two and dipped well into the junior ranks to promote promising young officers who were spoiling for a fight.

To get more officers for sea service, the Navy Department turned to the merchant marine. In 1861 Welles appointed a total of 993 masters, master's mates, paymasters, and engineers. These officers met high standards and were selected by examination. And, the Navy Department had to compete for enlisted personnel. State and local authorities were paying substantial bonuses for enlistment into the army. To obtain enough recruits, the Federal navy was also forced into a system of dollar attractions, some of which ran as high as one thousand dollars. These procurement policies were eminently successful. From a modest personnel strength of 6,700 sailors at the start of the war, the navy mustered over 51,000 men in April 1865.

Since, at the outbreak of the war, no one in the navy had prepared a plan for operations against the South, the Secretary appointed two boards of distinguished officers whom he trusted. The first was a strategy board headed by Captain Samuel Francis DuPont. Suave, courtly, a man of infinite social charm, DuPont was a member of the wealthy gunpowder manufacturing family. Having fought in the Mexican War, he had considerable experience in coastal blockade. His able assistants on the board were Professor Alexander Dallas Bache, Superintendent of the U.S. Coast Survey, Major J. G. Barnard, Corps of Engineers, U.S. Army, and Commander Charles Henry Davis, U.S. Navy. The recommendations of this board helped to shape the North's overall strategy for the remainder of the war.

Its first suggestion was to divide the Atlantic Squadron into two blockading squadrons, with a boundary line falling approximately between the coasts of North and South Carolina. Next, the board advised the establishment of a base near the southern end of the Atlantic coast to serve as a coaling and supply station. It also recommended that the Union navy attack selected strong points along the Southern coast and on inland waters. The board's last major recommendation, and the one which had a devastating effect on the South when it was realized, was to seize the Mississippi River and split the Confederacy in two.

[8]

These were daring and imaginative plans. Despite the fact that the South did not have a navy, the plans involved considerable danger for Union naval forces. At that time it was the current military belief that one gun in a shore emplacement was the equal to five guns on a ship. To carry out this recommended strategy, the navy would have to bombard forts in uncharted waters and operate in confined rivers. Neither side had much experience in river warfare. Following the European military principle of holding inland waterways "from the bank," the Confederates erected a "chain of forts" along their largest rivers. The Union navy had to improvise and it used all sorts of expedients, but from the beginning it adopted a naval, or at least an amphibian, strategy. The willing cooperation between the Union army and navy in river warfare and in coastal invasion was the chief reason for their many victories.

Meanwhile, Secretary Welles' second board was deliberating a matter of utmost importance. The ironclad board, headed by Commodore Joseph Smith, had been formed as a matter of necessity. It was no secret that the Confederates had raised the hulk of the Yankee frigate *Merrimac* from its bed of mud in Norfolk, and were working day and night to refit her as an ironclad. The Secretary of the Confederate navy, Stephen R. Mallory, originally intended that the *Merrimac* be used as an iron ram to break the blockade in Hampton Roads. He ordered the Norfolk Navy Yard to concentrate on the *Merrimac* "at the expense and delay of every other work on hand if necessary."

At a special session of Congress in late July 1861, Welles had pleaded the case for ironclads in the U.S. Navy and won approval to appoint a board to investigate their use. Congress appropriated one and a half million dollars for ironclad construction. This set off a race in technical development that went right down to the wire and ended in a tie. In March 1862 the North's little *Monitor* arrived at Hampton Roads, Virginia, to challenge *Merrimac* scant hours after that Confederate ironclad had terrorized the Union blockading fleet. In its day, the ironclad represented a "quantum jump" in naval warfare, having as much overall effect then as the Polaris missile submarine has today.

With his expansion program moving at full speed, and having a well-charted course in front of him, Secretary Welles was now ready to move. The Union navy was eager for action and was willing to carry out the war along the lines agreed upon in the dingy halls of the Navy Department. As we shall see, it did the job with little fanfare, but with telling effectiveness.

TWO

⚓

Early Losses

FORT SUMTER

THE winter of 1860–61 was one of uncertainty and watchful waiting. The seven "cotton states" of the South were busily forming a
new government at Montgomery, Alabama, while President Buchanan searched for some way to win them back into the Union. At
the same time he had to maintain a delicate political balance with
the remaining seven slaveholding states—Virginia, Maryland, North
Carolina, Tennessee, Kentucky, Arkansas, and Missouri—to prevent
them from joining the Confederacy. No one knew what to expect or
what might happen as the confused winter dragged to an end.
Trains continued to run between the North and South and businessmen found ways to conduct their affairs across borders. People in
the seceded states continued to use U.S. stamps on their letters.
Perhaps it was symbolic of the times that as late as March 1861 the
New York and Savannah steamers were still running, carrying the
United States flag at the peak and the Confederate flag at the fore.

But the days of business-as-usual and ships flying two flags were
numbered. The catalyst which exploded this uncertainty and projected a divided country into its bloodiest war was a masonry fort
at the entrance of South Carolina's Charleston Harbor.

Fort Sumter, one of the nation's first "pentagons," was almost a
joke in 1860; Charlestonians were willing to wager that it would
crumble with age before it was finished. Thirty-one years had elapsed
since the government had appropriated half a million dollars and
had commenced building an artificial island of granite as the foundation of a large brick fort to guard that important seaport. True, by

1860 the masonry shell had been completed, but a great deal of work still remained before the fort could be garrisoned or gunned. In June, Congress appropriated funds for the completion of Fort Sumter and the repair of nearby Fort Moultrie. Captain John G. Foster, U.S. Army Corps of Engineers, arrived in September to complete the job. Unable to find enough skilled workmen in Charleston, Foster sent to Baltimore for workers and soon the harbor bustled with building activity.

As the repairs to Fort Sumter proceeded, a succession of events brought the United States on the verge of conflict during the last months of President Buchanan's term of office. When South Carolina seceded from the Union on December 20, 1860, Governor Francis W. Pickens sent commissioners to Washington to claim possession of the forts in Charleston Harbor and to reach an agreement regarding all public property in the state. On the day after Christmas, the commander of the U.S. Army detachment in Fort Moultrie, Major Robert H. Anderson, electrified North and South alike by evacuating Moultrie and moving his force into Fort Sumter.

A West Point graduate of the class of 1825, Anderson was fifty-five years old and still a major despite his brilliant thirty-five-year military career. A thorough man, Anderson had sought out the best advice in Washington before he went to Charleston to take command. He called on General Winfield Scott, the Army general in chief, and learned from the experienced old soldier that Fort Moultrie was indefensible against land attack. This opinion was confirmed by Captain George W. Cullum, an engineering officer who had spent the past five years working on Fort Sumter and improving Charleston Harbor. Cullum believed that Fort Sumter would be the only safe place for Northern troops in Charleston, and that all other forts which were accessible by land could be taken easily in the event of conflict.

On December 23, when Governor Pickens' emissaries took the train to Washington, Major Anderson felt that this was the final peaceful overture. He believed rightly that, if negotiations failed, South Carolina would settle the matter by force of arms. While he

hoped that the act of moving his troops to Sumter would help preserve the peace, he knew full well that in the troubled situation a
single mishap might bring on war. Accordingly, he kept his counsel
and did not tell any of his officers or men that he had decided to
make the move on Christmas Day. Bad weather caused him to reluctantly postpone his operation one more day.

On December 26 Anderson moved his garrison at dusk to avoid
discovery by harbor guard boats. His troops occupied Fort Sumter
with fixed bayonets, driving back the curious crowd of workmen that
met them on the wharf. The whole move was beautifully executed,
much to the chagrin of Charlestonians in general, and Governor
Pickens in particular. That evening Major Anderson reported to the
Secretary of the Army that he had spiked the guns at Fort Moultrie,
burned the gun carriages, and was now firmly established in Fort
Sumter with one year's medical stores and a four months' supply of
provisions.

In the resulting turmoil at Washington, President Buchanan and
his cabinet deliberated for four days to determine a course of action.
Anderson was called both traitor and hero in the same breath. To
say the least, he had rocked Buchanan's boat and forced the President into a ticklish situation which demanded a decision of the
moment—not postponement until President-elect Lincoln should relieve him. The North was so aroused that Buchanan feared impeach-
ment. He told a friend confidentially, "If I withdraw Anderson from
Sumter, I can travel home to Wheatland by the light of my own
burning effigies." Reluctantly, therefore, he informed the commissioners from South Carolina that Fort Sumter would be defended,
but added that this did not mean that such a defense should be
construed as a menace to the city of Charleston.

Governor Pickens' immediate reaction to Anderson's move was to
occupy Castle Pickney, a small brick fort a few hundred yards off
the Charleston waterfront. Later his state troops seized Fort
Johnson, a quarantine station flanking the harbor channel. This set
off a chain reaction around the whole Southern coastline. In the
next ten days forts in Savannah, St. Augustine, Mobile Bay, and Pensacola were taken over by local state troops. By mid-January, only

Fort Sumter in Charleston and Fort Pickens at Pensacola remained firmly in Union hands.

It was obvious to the leaders in Washington that Fort Sumter, although it held a strong position against Confederate attack, was indeed a liability unless it could be reinforced and provisioned by sea. Anderson's supply of provisions became one of the controlling factors of ensuing developments. General Scott was the first to suggest a relief expedition. In one of his peculiar third-person notes, he informed President Buchanan that, "It is Sunday; the weather is bad and General Scott is not well enough to go to church. But matters of the highest national importance seem to forbid a moment's delay, and if misled by zeal, he hopes for the President's forgiveness. Will the President permit General Scott, without reference to the War Department and otherwise, as secretly as possible, to send two hundred and fifty recruits from New York Harbor to reinforce Fort Sumter . . .?" The President agreed and General Scott made plans to send the troops on the *Brooklyn* which, with its twenty-five guns, could force an entrance into Charleston Harbor if necessary.

Meanwhile President Buchanan began to vacillate again; he informed Scott that it would not be "honorable" to use a warship for this mission and that he preferred to use a private merchant steamer instead. Shortly thereafter, the steamer *Star of the West* was chartered at twelve hundred and fifty dollars a day. It was loaded with troops in the dark of night near Staten Island in New York Harbor, and sent on its mission in the greatest secrecy. The troops were actually told to "hide below decks" upon entering Charleston. But the news leaked out through Secretary Jacob Thompson of Buchanan's cabinet and Anderson learned of the forthcoming relief expedition through the Charleston newspapers. In the first light of dawn on January 9, the *Star of the West* steamed boldly in the channel toward Fort Sumter, passing between Confederate batteries on Morris Island to the south, and Fort Moultrie to the north.

The Carolinians were ready, especially a young Citadel cadet named George E. Haynsworth from the city of Sumter, South Carolina. His was the first shot of the secession. The cannonball arced over the *Star of the West* without damage, but it was immediately followed by others. In spite of two light hits, the *Star of the West* continued up the channel out of range of the Morris Island battery and approached the more formidable guns at Fort Moultrie. Here a moment of truth arose for Major Anderson. His guns could have silenced those of Moultrie, but in his indecision he would not give the order to fire. The relief ship, noting that Fort Sumter was not protecting it from the fire of Fort Moultrie, turned back in desperation and headed out of the harbor.

When the *Star of the West* left in disgrace, Governor Pickens set about improving Confederate defenses, for he knew full well that an armed ship of the Union navy could have forced the relief of Sumter and would have succeeded where the *Star of the West* failed. Through the months of January and February the situation remained unchanged, but with the inauguration of Lincoln on March 4, the Union attitude shifted. On his second day as President, Lincoln learned that Anderson would soon be starved into surrender if nothing more were done, so he decided to force a decision.

At this point Gus Fox entered the picture. An ex-naval officer of burning energy and ambition, he begged for a chance to reconnoiter Charleston Harbor to see if relief from the sea was still feasible. This was granted. When Fox returned he reported that he would put troops on board a large steamer, hire two powerful New York tugboats, and under the protection of the *Pawnee* and the revenue cutter *Harriet Lane,* he would relieve Fort Sumter if the reluctant Major Anderson would do his part. Secretary Welles promptly approved the plan and issued sailing orders on April 5. With his characteristic New England caution, Welles also added the screw sloop *Powhatan* to Fox's force, not realizing that this change would doom the enterprise to failure.

On April 8, the *Harriet Lane* sailed from New York for Fort Sumter, and was followed the next day by Gus Fox in the steamer *Baltic. Pawnee* left Hampton Roads on April 10, joined the other ships, and arrived off Charleston Harbor on the morning of April 12. Here the frustrated Fox waited in vain for *Powhatan,* while Confederate guns boomed the attack on Fort Sumter.

Unknown to Fox or Secretary Welles, President Lincoln had

agreed to form a second relief expedition to reinforce Fort Pickens at Pensacola. This action had preempted the *Powhatan* from Fox's command four days earlier, but no one knew about it except a lieutenant named David Dixon Porter, two other military officers, and Secretary of State Seward. When the *Powhatan* sailed from New York to precede the relief force to Sumter, Porter was concealed in a cabin. As the ship steamed by Staten Island, Porter made himself known to the captain and showed him an order signed by President Lincoln which gave Porter command of the ship. By this amateur "cloak-and-dagger" act, the *Powhatan*'s captain learned that he had lost his command. He was put ashore in New York and Porter promptly changed the ship's destination from Charleston to Pensacola.

The day before Fox arrived at Charleston, the Confederate government had wired Brigadier General Pierre G. T. Beauregard to demand Fort Sumter's surrender. When Major Anderson refused, orders from Montgomery instructed Beauregard to "reduce the fort as your judgment decides to be most practical." The artillery commander had acted accordingly. At midnight on the eleventh he alerted his batteries and commenced the fateful bombardment at 4:30 A.M. the next morning. The Union fort soon became a place of reverberating thunder, filled with flying chunks of broken masonry and pieces of metal.

Fox was in a quandary. He had arrived off Charleston too late, and his strongest ship had been taken from him. To make matters worse, the other ship commanders had orders which required them to wait for *Powhatan* before entering the harbor. The disappointed Fox could only watch as Confederate land batteries battered away at the walls of Fort Sumter.

A Union soldier inside the fort recorded in his diary, "We all think that we shall be able to stand it for about ten days. They cannot take the fort by assault unless they wish to sacrifice from three to four thousand lives. It is impossible to think that they should enter the fort." Although they did not hold out for ten days, to their credit they resisted manfully and kept up a return fire until their ammunition ran low, the barracks on fire, and their food all but gone. Ultimately Anderson agreed to accept Beauregard's terms to cease fire. He was permitted to salute the United States flag, and then embark on Fox's ships waiting outside the channel entrance.

Damage on both sides was light. The only fatality caused by fire from Fort Sumter's guns was a horse on Morris Island. Four Confederates in Fort Moultrie suffered slight wounds, and four men in Sumter itself were scratched by flying debris. More than three thousand shot and shell had been thrown at Sumter by Beauregard's batteries, six hundred of which scored direct hits on the masonry walls. The fort was a shambles after the battle but its basic defenses were intact. Sumter was still a formidable defense which was to serve the Confederacy well against later Union efforts to take Charleston from the sea.

Oddly enough, it was Anderson's final salute to the flag which produced the only casualties of the battle. He fired a salute of fifty guns on the afternoon of April 14 while thousands of Charlestonians celebrated their victory. In the middle of the salute something went wrong on one of the barbette guns and a tremendous explosion ripped through the parapet. Private Hough was killed instantly and five other men were wounded. The tragedy cut short the salute and delayed the evacuation, while sorrowful Union soldiers held funeral ceremonies for Private Hough in the Sumter parade ground.

The episode at Fort Sumter in 1861 welded the North into one patriotic force, having about the same effect upon the country as the Japanese attack on Pearl Harbor eighty years later. Major Robert Anderson became the "Galahad of the North," whose stubborn defense had created a hysterical national spirit overnight. While he himself was crushed with a sense of failure, he was feted and lauded by his admirers. Lincoln commissioned him a brevet major general, and in that capacity Anderson returned four years later on Good Friday, April 14, to raise the flag of the United States once again over the battered walls of Fort Sumter.

Norfolk Navy Yard

In the first critical weeks of his administration, President Lincoln continued to mollify and appease the uncommitted Southern border states. Before the attack on Fort Sumter there was every reason to believe that some of these states would remain within the Union. To avoid an upset, Lincoln advised all cabinet members to refrain from steps that might arouse suspicion or cause needless alarm. These tactics seemed successful; in spite of the feverish activities of the Confederacy to organize a Southern government in Montgomery, the seven slaveholding states near the border did not budge. An encouraging event occurred in early April when the Virginia State Delegation met in Richmond and voted to remain with the Union.

Navy Secretary Gideon Welles was unimpressed by Virginia's action, and felt that trouble was brewing nevertheless. Still mindful of Lincoln's desires to avoid overt moves, he proceeded cautiously and secretly to take preliminary steps to protect ships and navy property in the South. He remembered well the lessons of January when almost every military post of any importance in the seceded states had been seized by state militia.

The navy's largest and most productive shipyard south of the Mason-Dixon Line was in a tenuous position. The Norfolk Navy Yard was located on the Elizabeth River close by the city of Portsmouth, Virginia. Founded by the British in the late 1600's, it had been confiscated by Virginians during the Revolutionary War, and was purchased later from England by the U.S. government in 1801. With its long history and thriving naval repair work, it had become an integral and important part of the Norfolk community.

The Norfolk Navy Yard was one of the most valuable properties of the Union navy. It contained modern machine shops, boiler shops and foundries, sail lofts, carpenter shops, and a large dry dock. In addition to this capable industrial plant, it boasted the country's largest arsenal and reserve supply of naval guns. The yard storage contained over one thousand guns of all description, some obsolete, but included were about three hundred pieces known as "Dahlgrens." These were the most modern guns of the times. They were built in the Naval Gun Factory under Captain John A. B. Dahlgren's specifications, which featured the new principle of the curve of pressures. The largest and most formidable of these were nine inches in diameter, and fifty-two of them were in the Norfolk storage.

In April there were many vessels at the yard. Some of them had been tied up to the wharves without crews for several years. Included were sailing sloops, frigates, and old ships of the line. However, the most important of all was the steam frigate *Merrimac*—a fifty-gun screw-propelled ship which had been built in Boston six years earlier. The *Merrimac* was worth all the rest of the ships put together, but unfortunately she was undergoing overhaul and was unable to steam on her own power.

At the same time that the Virginia State Convention had voted to remain loyal, there were alarming rumors in Washington about the growth of the Old Dominion Secessionist Party. These alarms caused Secretary Welles to alert the commander of the Norfolk Navy Yard on April 10 to prepare the USS *Merrimac* for transfer to a Northern port. He warned that "great vigilance should be exercised in guarding and protecting the public interests committed to your charge."

Welles ordered Commander James Alden to take command of the *Merrimac,* and sent Chief Engineer Benjamin F. Isherwood to Norfolk to put the ship's engines back in commission as soon as possible. On April 16, after news of Fort Sumter had electrified the North, Welles wrote to Flag Officer G. J. Pendergrast, who commanded the USS *Cumberland* at Norfolk to defer his scheduled departure for Veracruz. He directed Pendergrast to assist "towards putting the vessels now in the Yard in condition to be moved, placing the ordnance and ordnance stores on board for moving, and in case of invasion, insurrection, or violence of any kind to suppress it, repelling assault by force, if necessary." This was a large order which caught many naval officers by surprise, for they had not believed that their new secretary would undertake such a daring plan.

Isherwood returned to Washington on the eighteenth and reported in disgust that after he had reassembled *Merrimac's* engineering plant, he was ordered by Commodore McCauley to put out the fires under the boilers. Convinced that McCauley was now ineffective and completely under the influence of the Southern-sympathizing officers on his staff, Secretary Welles ordered Commodore Hiram Paulding to proceed to Norfolk and take command of all the naval forces there afloat. Welles also charged his new commander that

under no circumstances should he allow guns and munitions to "fall into the hands of insurrectionists," advising him to repel them by force if necessary to carry out those orders, and giving him permission to destroy naval ships and materiel at Norfolk if required.

It took Paulding two days to assemble a force of one hundred marines and the necessary gunpowder and inflammables. He arrived in Norfolk in the afternoon of April 20, stopping at Fort Monroe to pick up a detachment of army troops before he proceeded up the Elizabeth River to the navy yard. On his arrival he relieved Commodore McCauley, but not before the panicky old commander had ordered men to spike the *Merrimac's* guns and scuttle the ship. Paulding's inexperienced marines and emergency crews tried to save the *Merrimac* but they were too late.

Paulding then took stock of his situation. His marines knew nothing about ships and would be of little value in moving them to safety. On the other hand his force was too small to defend the yard against the growing groups of state militia outside the navy yard gates. He decided to fall back on the most drastic of his instructions—to destroy installations and ships rather than let them fall into Secessionist hands. By this decision the Union navy dealt itself the severest blow that it would receive during the whole four years of war. Secretary Welles lived to regret this precipitous action which destroyed over two million dollars' worth of yard property, several serviceable ships, and gave hundreds of cannons to the Confederacy.

Having made up his mind to destroy rather than defend, Paulding proved to be a poor arsonist. He sent a group under his executive officer, Charles Wilkes, to fill the *Merrimac* and neighboring ships with combustibles. Another force of men put mines at the dry dock gates, while a third tended to the shops, barracks, and warehouses. Powder trains were laid so that the fire could be ignited on a given signal. While these preparations were going on, a detachment of troops and marines were unsuccessfully trying to destroy guns and cannons with sledgehammers.

Crowds outside the yard gates grew sullen as lookouts described the unusual activity taking place behind the walls. A premature fire

in one of the barracks lit up the scene and caused a hasty withdrawal of fire brigades to the ships. Commodore Paulding was about to fire a rocket as a signal to light the powder trains, when Commodore McCauley's youngest son came to him with tears in his eyes and reported that the old gentleman would not leave his post. Commander Alden went to the commandant's quarters and persuaded him to come aboard the sloop *Cumberland,* which had been made ready for towing. Shortly after 4 A.M. Paulding sent off his rocket signal. Sheets of flame roared skyward, and angry Virginia militiamen broke through the gates to save what they could.

A group of Confederates under the leadership of one of McCauley's former officers managed to flood the dry dock before the mines could explode. They saved many other vital installations of the yard, including the valuable store of naval ordnance. According to Admiral Porter, guns for the batteries and fortifications erected on Southern coasts and rivers came almost exclusively from the Norfolk Yard.

Paulding was more successful in his effort to burn the Union ships. With their seasoned wood and pitchy decks these vessels made an elaborate bonfire, burning to the water's edge and settling on the bottom. Most of the *Merrimac* was saved when it settled in the water; it suffered fire damage only in the superstructure and upper decks. The hull and engines were intact and were essentially the same when the ship later sailed under a Confederate flag as the first ironclad to see action.

The only ship actually saved was sailing sloop *Cumberland,* which Paulding put under tow astern of the tug *Yankee.* The *Cumberland* grounded on an obstruction in the channel near Craney Island, but it was pulled off afterward by the *Keystone State* and *Yankee.* Paulding put the *Cumberland* in a safe anchorage in Hampton Roads near Fort Monroe's batteries, and proceeded to Washington in the *Pawnee* to make his report.

The destruction of the Norfolk Navy Yard was viewed by a Congressional Committee of Investigation as one of the greatest calamities of the war. Destruction was bad enough, but the loss of guns which could be turned against the North was worse. The mood in the Capitol at the end of April was one of unhappy frustration. First Sumter and then Norfolk had fallen. When this was followed by the defeat at Bull Run (Manassas, Virginia) in July, Lincoln pleaded with Secretary Welles for a naval victory to cheer a despairing nation.

⚓

THREE

The Union Blockade

THE Union blockade of the Confederacy was ordered in haste and proclaimed in confusion. It was viewed at first by foreign countries as a remarkable evidence of ignorance or stupidity on the part of Lincoln's administration. This ill-advised start can be traced to Secretary of State William Henry Seward, author of the proclamation, who had previously demonstrated carelessness in naval matters.

European statesmen were puzzled by the use of the word "blockade." A country having internal difficulties on the order of an insurrection or a rebellion would "close" its ports. Under international law a blockade is a recognized act of war between two independent and belligerent nations. Thus Lincoln's order was equivalent to recognition of the South as a separate belligerent nation which was entitled to many rights under historic usage of international law. Throughout the war, Secretary Welles made frequent bitter references in his diary about this aspect of the President's edict.

Lincoln proclaimed the blockade of the six seceded Southern states on April 19, 1861, declaring that "a competent force will be posted so as to prevent the entrance and exit of the vessels from the ports aforesaid." This first proclamation was issued five days after the evacuation of Fort Sumter, and coincided with the burning of the Norfolk Navy Yard. Eight days later, for a reason that is difficult for historians to pin down, the President issued a second proclamation extending the blockade to include the states of North Carolina and Virginia, neither of which had yet seceded from the Union! Tidewater statesmen demanded, "Why, and by what right had he blockaded the coasts of states which were still a part of the Union?" This untimely action stirred a wave of protest and was one of the primary reasons why North Carolina and Virginia seceded shortly thereafter.

The general Southern attitude to the proclamations was first one of anger, but it later turned to disdain and amusement. How could the North possibly blockade thirty-five hundred miles of coastline with its small navy? Moreover, the Treaty of Paris, to which the United States subscribed, stated that a blockade had to be effective before it would be recognized by other nations. Consequently, Lincoln and his Navy Secretary had their work cut out for them. To issue or proclaim a blockade was one thing, but to enforce it was another.

Secretary Welles admittedly had a poor start for the action that is now recorded as the greatest blockade in naval history. It was an almost impossible task. The distance from Cape Henry to the Rio Grande was greater than the distance from New York to London; the coast was punctured by 189 rivers and thousands of inlets. The double coastline off the coasts of North Carolina and Virginia, the Sea Islands off Georgia, the treacherous Florida Keys, as well as the swamps and deltas of the Gulf Coast added to Welles' troubles and required literally hundreds of ships for proper patrol. However, Welles' naval aides noted that in spite of the great distance to cover, the number of primary blockade targets was manageable. There were many small ports and hamlets on inlets and rivers, but there were only ten Southern ports that had good connections with the interior by either river or rail. If the Union navy could stop traffic into Norfolk, Beaufort, New Bern, Wilmington, Charleston, Savannah, Pensacola, Mobile, New Orleans, and Galveston, it would halt all but a trickle of imported goods.

Using the "rifle" instead of a "shotgun" approach helped, but the blockade still had growing pains. Not only were there insufficient ships to establish an effective patrol, but also Union naval officers were untrained in this kind of duty. They were not sure of their ground when they stopped a suspect flying a foreign flag, nor did they have enough experienced personnel to put aboard a captured ship in order to take it to a prize court. Thus the Union navy's blockade was necessarily a "paper" blockade at first, with ships stationed on patrol more as a gesture than a threat. But the blockade force grew rapidly, took on an efficient organization, and the crews learned their business in a short time.

Gideon Welles obtained authority from the President to charter or purchase enough vessels for the naval service to close the Rebel ports. The navy grew in leaps and bounds. Ferryboats, fishing boats, whalers, and yachts joined steamers, freighters, and naval warships to enlarge the blockade forces. As fast as Welles could commission and arm these ships, he would send them South. In the first eight months of the war he purchased and armed 118 ships of all descriptions. Marine shipyards turned out 23 gunboats in less than three months. The "90-day" gunboats, as they were affectionately called, were not very formidable, carrying only four guns of small caliber, but they had nothing to fear from the nonexistent Confederate navy. They were excellent boats for pursuing blockade-runners in shallow waters and winding rivers.

The Secretary's frantic efforts brought results quicker than he had expected. By July 1861 there was a Union man-of-war off each major Southern port. Port authorities were notified of the effective date of the blockade and were advised that under international law neutral vessels would be given a fifteen-day period of grace in which to depart.

Welles' advisory boards recommended the establishment of area commanders in charge of blockades. The first of these was the Atlantic Blockade Squadron under command of Captain Silas Stringham. As the force grew it was further divided into the North Atlantic Squadron, the South Atlantic Squadron, the Eastern Gulf Squadron, the Western Gulf Squadron, the Mississippi Squadron, the Potomac Flotilla, and in late 1862 Welles stationed a Pacific Squadron which operated from a base at Mare Island, north of San Francisco. Almost every action of the Union navy in ensuing war years was in support of this giant blockade—although Secretary Welles released a few larger ships to hunt down Captain Raphael Semmes, whose commerce raids almost drove Union shipping from the seas.

In 1863, when the tightening blockade was likened to a giant anaconda squeezing the life out of the South, Welles was able to boast that not only did he have an effective force at sea, but that he also had a formidable force on the Confederate rivers. There were over one hundred ships employed in river patrol, cutting off Rebel supplies, and aiding the army. A stickler for statistics, Secretary Welles noted that the distance patrolled by gunboats on the Mississippi and its tributaries was 3,615 miles, and that the sounds, rivers, inlets, and bayous of the Atlantic and the Gulf Coast in which his gunboats operated was another 2,000 miles. In a masterpiece of understatement on the success of his blockade he said, "the stringency of the blockade has operated with great severity on those who have risen in arms against their country, and has caused heavy losses to those who have abetted, or have been in sympathy with the rebellion."

The North Atlantic Squadron watched and guarded the rivers and coast of Virginia and the sounds of North Carolina. It operated out of Hampton Roads from a secure anchorage near Fort Monroe, and had a fairly short haul from base to patrol. Wilmington was the most difficult port in this area. It was accessible from the sea by two separate channels about thirty miles apart, both of which were well guarded by Southern batteries. In his report at the end of 1863, Welles admitted that some fast light-draft Clyde steamers had penetrated the North Atlantic blockade, but that none had got by at Washington, New Bern, or the inland waters of North Carolina, nor had they been successful on the Nansemond, York, or other rivers of Virginia.

The South Atlantic Squadron had a more difficult task. At first the blockading units were required to steam all the way back to Norfolk for resupply, but amphibious landings gave the Union footholds in Hatteras, North Carolina, and Port Royal, a fine harbor just to the south of Charleston. That defiant city, "The Cradle of the Confederacy," repelled all attempts to capture it from the sea, and its well-placed batteries kept blockading ships out beyond the sandbar. However, once Union forces seized Morris Island, the combination of that island battery and the ring of ships outside effectively stopped all blockade-running. Welles could report in all honesty that in the last few months of 1863 not a single runner had penetrated the blockade at Charleston.

The coasts of Florida, from what is now called Cape Kennedy on the east to Pensacola on the west, were the responsibility of the Eastern Gulf Squadron. Unlike the other blockading units, this squadron was not required to support army operations and was able to concentrate solely on the blockade. This was fortunate, for the short run to Havana and Nassau was favored by many blockade-runners. In summarizing the work of this blockading squadron for 1863, Secretary Welles pointed out that Southern trade had suffered severely, and that over one hundred different craft had been captured or destroyed.

The job of the Western Gulf Squadron was perhaps the toughest. After the capture of New Orleans, Admiral David Farragut took most of his best ships up the Mississippi River, leaving the coastal blockade to a junior officer of his command. One of the knottiest problems in these waters was the illicit traffic up the Rio Grande, a river which Lincoln was reluctant to close because it served as the boundary line between the United States and Mexico. The Mexican port of Matamoros bustled with activity as long as the Rio Grande remained open, forcing the Union navy to finally occupy Brownsville, Texas. This move effectively closed off the river, and Matamoros' import business soon dropped to its small prewar level.

The Potomac Flotilla captured prizes on that river almost throughout the war. Welles pointed out how "mercenary adventurers as well as Rebels and Rebel sympathizers" carried out illicit trade between Maryland and Virginia, making it necessary to keep a considerable force on the Potomac. These attempts continued in spite of numerous interceptions by the flotilla, much to the irritation of Secretary Welles, who complained that the punishment for offenders was too light.

As the war dragged from one weary year to the next, the blockade continued through sweltering summers and freezing wintry gales. For the Confederates who ran the blockade, life was exciting, glamorous, and broken by frequent visits to ports where they were given a hero's welcome. But aboard the Union ships life was dull and hard. Strict general orders required blockaders to inspect each suspicious ship, approaching only when in full battle quarters and ready to fight. Compliance with these orders often forced crews to stand at battle stations for hours on end, with nothing to do but watch and wait. Frequently they would return from a long chase and tumble exhausted into their hammocks, only to be called again moments later when another hull showed over the horizon. Then the process would be repeated all over again. Unit commanders tried to improve the situation by proper attention to discipline, cleanliness, and morale. They inspected each ship once a quarter, and observed exercises at boarding, landing, and gunnery practice. The commanders required a taut watch at all times, but insisted that the crews be given time for recreation.

The day's routine was about the same that warships have used for centuries. Reveille was held at sunrise, decks were scrubbed before breakfast, then all hands were assembled at quarters for muster. This was followed by cleaning, polishing, drilling at ship's guns, watch standing, noon meal, and then a repetition of the morning's routine. After an early supper men would gather on the forecastle or some more sheltered spot in rough weather, and would listen to old sailors tell sea stories. They would sing and play whatever musical instruments they had on board, and talk about their next shore leave. Admiral DuPont, knowing the value of music, asked the Navy Department to recruit bands and send them to the blockading squadrons. However, music and improvised theatricals were not enough to stop complaints of the enlisted men. In their boredom many drank too much grog, causing the Congress in 1862 to pass a law stopping the men's grog ration.

As the first year of the blockade drew to a close, the Navy Department ordered an action which stirred considerable controversy—closing off Southern ports by sinking ships in the harbor entrances. Called by Lord Russell of Great Britain "a cruel plan, which would seem to imply despair of the restoration of the Union," it was viewed by the South as "barbarism, not to be tolerated by enlightened governments." Simply stated, Welles' plan called for loading old wooden ships with stone and sinking them across the main channels of selected Confederate ports.

Decrepit whaling vessels located in New England, barely seaworthy for the passage to Charleston and Savannah, were purchased by the Navy Department to become part of the infamous "Stone Fleet." A total of twenty-five of these old wrecks were loaded with New England stone and formed into convoys. The ship's captains received sealed orders which were not to be opened until the ships were well out to sea. This precaution seemed unnecessary because Northern newspapers were giving accurate progress reports on the "Stone Fleet." The captains were advised to travel in company with their escorts, to show lights at night, and in case of fog near the coast to sound horns or bells. The orders continued, "You will also examine daily the pipe in the quarter of your ship under water to see that it remains safe." This referred to a pipe that had been installed to aid scuttling. It was a five-inch lead pipe fitted in a hole that had been bored through the ship's hull. In addition each crew was supplied with a giant auger to bore more holes if necessary. After the whaling captains delivered their ships to the blockade commander, they were given safe passage home in navy ships.

Professional naval officers regarded the "Stone Fleet" as sheer folly and beneath their dignity. Flag Officer DuPont wrote, "the Stone Fleet are all here at Savannah, and I hardly know what to do with them . . ." Nevertheless Secretary Welles was adamant, so his orders were carried out. On December 17, seven of the "Stone Fleet" vessels were sunk at the entrance to Savannah Harbor, and the remaining ships were sent to the bottom of the channel at Charleston on December 20.

Fortunately the "Stone Fleet" was a dismal failure, so neither the South nor England became ill-tempered. As the professional officers had pointed out, the ships could not be sunk with accuracy, and in the shifting sands of tidewater harbors, were quite harmless after they went to the bottom.

As ship after ship joined the regular Union blockading force, the cordon about the South drew tighter. No longer did sailboats and slow schooners slip by undermanned and inexperienced blockaders. Blockade-running soon became a dangerous occupation, but it was one which paid off so handsomely that it drew many an experienced captain, and enticed adventurous businessmen to invest in sleek, swift steamers. Indeed, blockade-running became a glamorous sport which was likened to a game of hare and hounds. Successful captains of blockade-runners became notorious idols who were lionized on completion of each successful passage. The most famous ship in the early stages of the blockade was the British mail steamer *Theodora*, skippered by a former British naval officer, Commander Lockwood. It was the *Theodora* who carried Confederate agents Mason and Slidell through the blockade at Charleston Harbor to Havana, where they transferred later to the British mail packet *Trent*. The subsequent incident between the USS *San Jacinto* and the *Trent* will be discussed later.

Four main ports served as neutral points for trans-shipment of goods: Nassau, Havana, Bermuda, and Matamoros. These sleepy little harbors soon burgeoned with bales of cotton, tobacco, English cannon, muskets and ammunition, silks and foodstuffs. The swift blockade-runners discharged their cargo, loaded again with goods from European merchants, and headed back for a Confederate port. Conventional freighters then picked up the exchange cargoes at the neutral port and sold them in Europe at great profit.

The blockade-runners were fast and short-legged. Their skippers knew every inch of the coast near the principal Southern ports, and were capable of making landfalls through fog or the blackest night. The little ships steamed darkened, and timed their voyage to arrive off port on a moonless night at high tide. They employed every ruse then known, and even invented some new ones. They chose the time and the place to break the blockade, used false signals, foreign flags, and local knowledge of rocks and shoals to their best advantage.

Only a few of the blockade-runners were owned by the Confederate government, which was understandably lax in establishing regulations for traffic in and out of its ports. Records show that the Union blockading fleet captured or destroyed a total of fifteen hundred ships that tried to run the blockade during 1861–65. Most of the civilian-owned boats dealt in luxuries for high profit, a point often overlooked by Southerners after the war who preferred to remember the gallant officers of the Confederate navy who ran the blockade. The "Prince of the Blockade-Runners" was Captain John

Newland Maffitt, a former officer of the Union navy who resigned to become the South's greatest blockade-runner. Close on his heels in fame was a brother officer, likewise trained first in the U.S. Navy, Captain John Wilkinson, intrepid skipper of the *Robert E. Lee.* The story of these two colorful figures is worth repeating.

The "Prince of the Blockaders" went to sea as a midshipman when he was thirteen years old. After he had served loyally in the U.S. Navy for nineteen years, John Maffitt joined some three hundred officers who "went South" in 1861. Of his nineteen years of naval service, fourteen were spent surveying the Atlantic coast with the United States Coastal Survey, concentrating on the coasts of the Carolinas. He became perhaps the world's best authority on the tricky currents, shoals, and tides of that tidewater section. In 1861 when he was commanding officer of USS *Crusader,* he demonstrated firmness and loyalty to his command by defying ardent secessionists in Mobile, and threatened to fire on them if they molested his ship. Later in the year he was ordered to New York and relieved. Proceeding to Washington, he learned of the firing on Fort Sumter and President Lincoln's proclamation of blockade and, on April 28, after much soul-searching, he resigned his commission in the U.S. Navy and went to Mobile to offer his services to the Confederacy.

After a short tour as naval aide to General Robert E. Lee, Maffitt was given command of the *Cecile,* an unusually fast ship with a capacity for about seven hundred bales of cotton. In her maiden voyage as a blockade-runner, *Cecile* received heavy fire from Union ships guarding Wilmington, but Maffitt's renowned luck saw him through the entire force safely to Nassau. He returned to the Carolina coast to survive another brush with blockaders, and won a daring chase through unmarked waters to the friendly port of Smithville. From January through April of 1862, Maffitt repeated his early success, bringing in quantities of arms, ammunition, medical supplies, and clothing for the Confederacy.

In May he was asked to take command of a Confederate gunboat that had been sent to Nassau from England. He waited out the long Caribbean summer for a court decision to release the ship to his custody. When he finally left Nassau in the unarmed, newly christened *Florida,* he located some guns, but was unable to get them into condition for firing because of a shortage of rammers, sponges, sights, and locks. Yellow fever erupted on the *Florida* and sickened most of her crew. Ill himself and barely able to stand, Maffitt nevertheless determined to take the *Florida* to Mobile where he could obtain the missing gun parts and get the ship into shape for commerce raiding. His drive through the Mobile Blockade Squadron in this unarmed ship cost him many casualties but it was hailed as one of the most daring exploits of the time.

In January 1863, with the *Florida* properly fitted out, he broke through the blockade again in hairbreadth fashion, and began a long cruise of destruction. Maffitt left the *Florida* in France after a heart attack had put him on the sick list, but in the spring of 1864 he was back again running the blockade, this time in the *Lillian,* a trim, fast steamer which had been built in Glasgow. Later he shifted to the government-owned *Owl,* and ended the war with a record of success unchallenged for length, the number of penetrations through the blockade, and for narrow escapes.

The intrepid John Wilkinson, first captain of the most famous of all the blockade-runners, the sleek *Robert E. Lee,* made up in daring what he may have lacked in local knowledge of the tidewater coast. His career started dismally enough when he was captured by Farragut's forces at the Battle of New Orleans. After several months' confinement in Fort Warren at Boston, he was exchanged for a Northern officer. He made his way to Richmond where Confederate Secretary Stephen R. Mallory picked him for a special blockade-running assignment. He gave Wilkinson sufficient funds and ordered him to proceed to England and purchase a fast vessel, load her with arms and supplies, and then return to a Confederate port as quickly as possible.

Captain Wilkinson made his way to England via Nassau, and found the very ship he wanted in Glasgow. She was the *Giraffe,* a Clyde-built side-wheeler that had been used in passenger runs between Glasgow and Belfast. Purchasing the *Giraffe* for $160,000, Wilkinson immediately stripped off all fancy cabins and unnecessary fittings, loaded his cargo, and made his way to Nassau. There he picked up two civilian pilots—one for Charleston and one for Wilmington—and headed for Charleston. Arriving off Charleston in late December 1862, Wilkinson was furious when his pilot refused to take him any closer. Giving him up as a hopeless case, Wilkinson slipped up the coastline to Wilmington and sneaked in through the dead of night. Just when it looked as if the *Giraffe* would enter the harbor undetected, she ran onto a sandbar. Working frantically and silently, Wilkinson's crew managed to refloat the ship without arousing Union blockading ships a short distance away, and moved under the protection of friendly Confederate batteries before sunrise.

Giraffe was promptly rechristened the *Robert E. Lee* and assigned to blockade-running. Under Wilkinson's skilled command, the *Robert E. Lee* made a total of twenty-one successful penetrations of the Union blockade, carrying about seven thousand bales of cotton out, and bringing in tons of supplies for the Confederacy. Late in 1863 Wilkinson was detached for another secret mission, leaving the *Lee* in command of a civilian captain, who allowed her to be captured on his first trip.

Captain Wilkinson went on to many more adventures, including a commerce-raiding cruise in the shipping lanes off the Northern coasts. At the end of the war he was back running the blockade, which by this time had become a hazardous occupation indeed. The last Confederate port of entry was lost when Admiral David Dixon Porter captured Fort Fisher outside Wilmington, but news of this loss did not reach Wilkinson in the *Chameleon* at sea. He ran boldly toward the fort, almost into the waiting arms of the Union fleet, when he decided that something was wrong and turned seaward with two Federal cruisers in hot pursuit. Eluding these "hounds," the "hare" tried to enter at Charleston and was almost captured again. Completely frustrated, Wilkinson returned to Nassau and ended his career by taking the *Chameleon* to London for final sale and disposition.

Many fortunes were made by those who dared risk the dangers of blockade-running. Cotton worth eight cents a pound in Dixie brought sixty in England, while drugs, clothes, guns, and ammunition were worth their weight in gold in the South. Trade exchange was so favorable that a blockade-runner could pay for itself in just one successful voyage. The lure of riches and the urgent needs of the Confederacy caused eight thousand penetrations of the blockade in the four years of its existence. Naval records show that fifteen hundred of the runners were either captured or destroyed. Their value was estimated at $30 million, much of it British property. Large as this loss was monetarily, it was even greater in its effect upon the Confederacy, which waited in vain for each trickle of supplies for its poorly equipped armies.

The blockade invoked an age-old practice at sea which created sizeable fortunes for Union naval officers engaged in blockading. The custom of awarding prize money to the captors of an enemy ship was well established before the Civil War. According to the laws of prize, the officers and crew of the ship making the capture were entitled to a share of the proceeds coming from the sale of both the ship and cargo. The government usually took half, while the rest was divided among the captors in a strict formula according to pay and rank. The squadron commander got five per cent, and the fleet captain one per cent. The blockader's share was divided up into twenty equal lots. The commanding officer got three of these, and four were shared by the lieutenants, masters, and warrants; the midshipmen and petty officers divided six, and the remaining seven went to the crew.

Some of the prizes awarded for an afternoon's work were fabulous. The master of the tug *Aeolus* got $13,164 for capturing the SS *Hope*, his assistant engineer received $6,657 and the seamen pocketed over $1,000 apiece. A few days later *Aeolus* assisted in capturing *Lady Sterling* which brought half a million dollars in the condemnation court. Each seamen on *Aeolus* received $2,000 for his share in this adventure.

The real killings were made by the blockade commanders. Admiral Samuel Phillips Lee of the North Atlantic Blockade Squadron banked $109,689 in his years on patrol, and he was closely followed by Admiral David Dixon Porter with $91,528. During the entire war the Treasury Department paid out a total of $10,103,764 to navy men in prize money. This was one aspect of the blockade which tended to offset the grueling, monotonous duty. In a postwar magazine account of 1870, when the total amount of prize awards was public knowledge, the blockade of the Civil War was described as duty which appealed to the "Pride, Patriotism, and Pocket" of the Union navy.

Historians have found it impossible to measure the efficiency of the Union blockade in terms of the direct effects on the South and the ultimate collapse of the Confederacy. The Southern shipowners did not record their commercial manifests or arrival and departure reports for posterity. The records of the U.S. Navy are available in Washington, but the records that still remain in the South are scattered among a variety of state and local museums. There is little doubt, however, that the grim line of Union ships throttled off the lifeblood of trade which kept the Confederacy alive.

The effectiveness of these squadrons cannot be measured entirely by the number of ships seized, destroyed, or run onto the shore. They caused numerous cargoes to rot on the wharves of Havana, Nassau, and Bermuda, and stalemated many ships inside Southern ports. Further, the blockading squadrons terrorized Southern coasts with numerous "commando" raids and bombardments, causing mass migration away from the fertile tidewater section to the relative safety of the interior. This constant threat was called the "navy's spear in the back of the Confederacy." It tied down troops, guns, and ammunition for coastal defense throughout the war. Harassed Southerners constantly lived in fear of the deadly fire of bombarding ships, and wondered where the next strike would fall.

⚓

First Amphibious Landings

HATTERAS

THE summer of 1861 was a dreary one for the Union. Sleek blockade-runners broke through the Union navy's blockade at will, and made announcements of arrivals and departures in local newspapers. Confederate privateers began to roam the seas off the New England coast, capturing or burning ships engaged in coastal traffic and starting a panic among Northern shipowners. Meanwhile, there was little to cheer about ashore. General Irvin McDowell's attempted drive to Richmond had failed in disastrous defeat at Bull Run, and gloom settled over the country. Harassed government officials in Washington, searching for a victory to offset these disappointments, listened eagerly when Secretary Welles proposed seizure of Confederate forts at Hatteras and Port Royal.

Welles' plan made sense. The Union navy was virtually unopposed at sea; it could strike with devastating power and overwhelming superiority at almost any point along the Southern coast. Why not, the Secretary of the Navy argued, move in a medium where every advantage fell to the Union? The Navy Department wanted action anyway. The early losses at Sumter and at Norfolk Navy Yard still rankled. There were too few ships to blockade the entire Southern coast effectively, but there were enough to make these amphibious landings. President Lincoln and his cabinet wholeheartedly approved the navy plan.

Hatteras was a natural choice for the first blow. It was a thorn in the side of the Union and a death trap for Northern commerce. Three Confederate privateers operated out of Hatteras Inlet, making daily dashes to capture or destroy Northern merchant ships. Situated on the easternmost tip of the outer bank at Pamlico Sound, Cape Hatteras was a valuable Southern stronghold and the entrance to many fine ports. West of the outer bank, the mainland of North Carolina was well connected to the interior by rail and inland waterways. Confederate war trade thrived in this area, using passes through the outer bank. The best and deepest of these was Hatteras Inlet, which was guarded by Forts Clark and Hatteras. In August 1861 a detachment of North Carolina State Militia was hurriedly completing work on the fortifications, finishing off the walls of sand with a layer of heavy mud from nearby marshes. Fort Hatteras was twice the size of little Fort Clark; it had sufficient guns to fight small craft, but the fort was no match against larger men-of-war. Its complement of three hundred and fifty men from the Seventh North Carolina Volunteers rushed construction along the walls and anxiously waited for heavier guns that were supposed to be coming any day.

On August 26 the commander of naval forces for the expedition, Captain Silas Stringham, assembled his ships in Hampton Roads. These well-armed ships looked good to the army troops in Fort Monroe who were to go aboard as the landing force. There were two steam frigates, the *Minnesota* and the *Wabash*, three sloops, and two steamers. Altogether they carried 158 guns to challenge the 25 old pieces installed on the Confederate forts. Here was naval superiority in the traditional sense—a concentration of overwhelming power that was mobile and self-supporting. Chartered to accompany the naval force were two troop carriers, *Adelaide* and *George Peabody*. For some unknown reason a third charter was added. This was the ancient tug *Fanny*, formerly used for inland canal traffic and scarcely seaworthy for the open sea. Somehow it weathered the rough weather en route, and performed many useful jobs during the assault.

General Benjamin F. Butler, an elected congressman from Massachusetts who gave up his seat to accept a commission as a major general, embarked eight hundred and fifty men aboard the troop carriers in the afternoon, and reported to Captain Stringham that he was ready. Each man was supplied with ten days' rations and one hundred and forty rounds of ammunition. The fleet sailed around 3 P.M. with bands playing and with soldiers and sailors cheering. It was the Union's first large amphibious operation, and also the first use of a strategy that was to lead the North from one victory to another.

Confederate lookouts at Hatteras spotted the fleet as it approached the outer bank in the late afternoon of the twenty-seventh. Ship after ship was reported to the alarmed Confederate commander Colonel William Martin, who dispatched a messenger inland to bring reinforcements. Meanwhile, Stringham's ships retired seaward to prepare for the attack that was to begin at dawn.

Breakfast was served before first light on the twenty-eighth and landing operations commenced at 6:40. This proved to be more difficult than Butler and Stringham had expected. Heavy surf crashed and boomed on the sandy beaches, swamping boats and nearly drowning the three hundred soldiers who managed to get ashore. The landing party could have been repulsed by a small detachment of cadets, and it probably would have suffered that fate except for the protecting guns of the *Pawnee, Harriet Lane,* and *Monticello.* This cover force was so formidable in comparison with anything the Confederates had to oppose them that the landing was carried out without one rifle fired in opposition.

At 10 A.M. Stringham's bombardment force began a slow circle, just out of range of the fort's guns, and delivered a withering fire into the earthern defenses. His heavier frigates drew from twenty-one to twenty-three feet, greater than the depth of the channel, and therefore had to remain outside the sandbar. Their big guns rooted up the fort's embankments with heavy shells. Little Fort Clark was almost defenseless. Outgunned, hopelessly torn apart by the punishing bombardment, and threatened with a landing force less than two miles away, the Confederate leader decided to evacuate and make a run for Fort Hatteras. The garrison spiked the few serviceable guns remaining, and abandoned their little post.

When Stringham and Butler saw men leaving Fort Clark and running down the sandy spit toward Fort Hatteras, they knew that the North had won its first significant victory. Looking across the island toward Fort Hatteras, they noted that its Confederate flag was down, and hastily concluded that both forts had surrendered.

Captain Stringham gave the order to cease fire, and tired gun crews watched Colonel Max Weber lead his land detachment into Fort Clark. At 2:00 P.M. the Stars and Stripes flew proudly over that ruined fort. Shortly thereafter came one of those inexplicable incidents which frequently occur in the excitement of battle. Union ships in Hatteras Inlet resumed fire on Fort Clark, sending their own troops scampering to shelter. Before Stringham's frantic signals to cease fire were obeyed, the bombardment had destroyed a supply of stores left behind by the Confederates and had also inflicted one of the few casualties suffered by Union forces in the entire engagement.

With Fort Clark firmly in Union hands, Stringham detached the light-draft *Monticello* to proceed up the inlet and take possession of Fort Hatteras. However, the fort had not surrendered and was still full of fight. Confederates explained later that their flag had been ripped to rags by the wind and that they did not have any replacements. The unsuspecting *Monticello* picked her way cautiously through the winding channel and, as she rounded the spit head, ran suddenly into a brisk fire from Hatteras.

Captain John Gillis, commanding, was in a tight spot. If he grounded in the shallow inlet his ship would be blown to bits, but he kept cool and extracted *Monticello* from the trap by backing his engines and using the heavy swells to advantage. In the meantime, *Monticello* answered the fort's fire with her pivot gun and port battery. Stringham promptly resumed the bombardment with his main force and covered *Monticello*'s retreat. When that little ship was clear, Gillis reported that she had received several hits but none that caused personnel casualties.

When the frigates fired to cover *Monticello*, Union troops in Fort Clark had to run for cover once again. The frigate's gun line to Fort Hatteras passed right over the smaller fort, and some of the shot fell short. Harassed soldiers in Fort Clark evacuated hastily, voicing a few scathing comments about the Union navy.

As darkness fell the issue of battle was still in doubt. Union soldiers ashore spent part of the miserable night in the rain, but some slipped back to Fort Clark to repossess it. Anxious thoughts plagued the men. Could the Confederates obtain reinforcements during the night? Would they be killed or wounded the next day? What would they do about provisions? Everything had been ruined during their morning landing through the surf. The forlorn men dug shallow wells in the sand and drank the brackish water. They rounded up a few sheep which they barbecued over their campfires, and settled down to wait for dawn.

In Fort Hatteras Confederate spirits soared when Commodore Samuel Barron arrived with reinforcements. Barron, son of the James Barron who had killed the naval hero Stephen Decatur in a duel, was himself a veteran of the U.S. Navy. He had served twenty-six years before he resigned to join the Confederacy; six months before, he had commanded the frigate *Wabash,* whose guns were now turned against him.

The storm that threatened Cape Hatteras moved out to sea during the night and fighting resumed after sunrise on August 29. This time Stringham issued strict orders not to fire on Fort Clark. The fleet bombardment worked over Fort Hatteras with deadly accuracy. Shells from nine-, ten-, and eleven-inch guns burst about the fort every few seconds, but not a single return shot from the fort reached a Union ship. They were all comfortably out of range.

The Confederates withstood cruel punishment for three hours, after which Barron called a conference of officers to discuss surrender. The council was rudely interrupted when a chance shot passed through a ventilator and set fire to the fort's magazine. Concluding that it would be foolhardy to put the fire out while the bombardment continued, Barron ran up a white flag shortly after 11:00 A.M.

Union Colonel Weber led his detachment of troops into Hatteras to take the surrender, but stubborn Commodore Barron refused to surrender to an army officer who had taken no part in the fight. General Butler solved the problem with the tug *Fanny,* transporting Barron and two other Confederate officers to Stringham's flagship.

There Commodore Barron ended his short service under the Confederate flag and surrendered his sword to his old friend and former comrade-in-arms.

About seven hundred Confederate prisoners were put aboard *Minnesota* for transportation to a Union prison. Colonel Weber's troops took possession of the fort and remained there as Stringham and Butler departed. Stringham sailed for New York aboard the flagship *Minnesota*, while Butler stopped at Hampton Roads to report to General John E. Wool. Both commanders quickly took trains for Washington to persuade authorities to retain Hatteras as a base rather than destroy it—as their original orders had stipulated. Within eight hours after their arrival in Washington, Lincoln issued orders to hold the fort and to resupply the garrison.

The seizure of Hatteras was more than a one-sided victory for the Union navy. Throughout the North it cheered people at home and served as a general morale booster for the entire navy. Secretary Welles ordered a national salute fired at all navy yards, and confidently predicted that there were more victories ahead. The South was alarmed at this sudden knife thrust into the ribs of North Carolina; the Southern press clamored for more coastal protection, warning Confederate leaders that no guns or troops should leave coastal states as long as the Union fleet lurked over the horizon. From a strategic point of view, the North's seizure of Hatteras plugged an important hole to the Southern coastline, gave the Union navy a much-needed naval base, and pinned down Confederate forces that were needed in Virginia and Tennessee.

While official Washington rejoiced over the victory at Hatteras, Navy Department planners were busily preparing for the next step in their master plan. The advisory board had recommended capturing Southern ports one by one; Captain Stringham had reached Hatteras first, but preparations for an even larger expedition to Port Royal in South Carolina were already well underway. However, since neither the army nor the navy had had much experience in this kind of operation, this largest amphibian movement in United States' history met with one delay after another.

PORT ROYAL

The board's choice of Port Royal as the next target was dictated by practical constraints. Charleston was too well defended, and monitors needed to challenge Fort Sumter were only on the drawing board. In the meantime it was imperative to use the "old Navy" to establish another Southern base for the Atlantic coast blockade.

Port Royal looked promising. It was one of the best natural harbors on the coast for ships with less than eighteen-foot draft, and it could be defended by superior naval strength once it was taken. The roadstead at Port Royal Sound enters the sea about midway between Charleston and Savannah, where the Broad and Beaufort rivers converge to form an anchorage large enough to accommodate several hundred ships. An extremely valuable port to the Confederacy, Port Royal served as an excellent point for trans-shipping cargo. Small ships could steam up the Broad River to a junction in the Charleston-Savannah railroad. Riverboats could reach Charleston over a fifty-mile patchwork of rivers and inlets. In recognition of Port Royal's importance, the South Carolina militia defended the channel entrance from two fairly strong fortifications.

President Jefferson Davis of the Confederacy was a West Point graduate who believed in, and understood, land armies. His overall military strategy for the "War of Secession" centered on the Army of Northern Virginia. Consequently, he resisted demands from governors of South Carolina, North Carolina, and Georgia for cannon, ammunition, and troops to defend their coasts. In November 1861 Southern seaboard fortifications were poorly constructed and feebly defended. The garrisons were long on courage and short on supplies of guns and ammunition. To quiet the complaining governors, the Confederate War Department appointed General Robert E. Lee in command of the entire South Atlantic coast to bolster defenses against the threat from the sea.

Lee hastily completed an inspection of the beaches from North Carolina to Florida, and reported to Richmond, "We have no guns that can resist" the Union fleet. After Port Royal eventually fell, he erected many river obstructions and strengthened defenses in Charleston and Savannah. Before he was moved from the Atlantic seaboard to command troops in Virginia, he had accomplished enough to restore order and to calm the fears of the populace. However, Lee pointed out to the War Department in Richmond the great advantage that sea power gave the North. It was a strength, he said, that could be "thrown with great celerity against any point, and far outnumbers any force we can bring against it in the field."

Months of preparation were made for Port Royal. Secretary Welles appointed the senior member of his advisory board, Captain DuPont, to lead naval forces assigned to the expedition, and the Secretary of War chose General W. T. Sherman to head army units. To avoid any bad feeling between the services (which had been overemphasized at Hatteras by the press), Lincoln instructed both military departments to ensure "most effective and cordial cooperation between the commanders of the expedition."

The force gathered slowly in Hampton Roads during beautiful October weather. A total of about 75 ships finally sailed on October 29. In addition to the men-of-war, there were 20 colliers, 6 supply vessels, and 25 transports chartered for the army's landing force of 17,000 men. Army supplies included ten days' cooked rations, 1,500 horses, 8,000 bags of oats, wheelbarrows, wagons, hoes, lumber, cement, tons of ammunition, and 500 small boats for landing through the surf. Experienced coastal seamen were carried to handle the boats, and over 1,000 freed Negroes were taken along to work on fortifications. It was a splendid job of planning, but as usual in a job of this size there occurred one mistake which has been repeated in later wars. Someone loaded the small-arms ammunition aboard ship first and it ended up in the bottom of cargo holds, buried beneath tons of other supplies. When General Sherman learned this, loading had already been completed, and he was informed that it would take four days to dig the ammunition out. In desperation he turned to General Wool at Fort Monroe, who questioned the sanity and naiveté of those who had botched the job, but finally turned over 350,000 rounds of cartridges to the red-faced Sherman.

Although Captain DuPont's force sailed with sealed orders, enemy speculation was quite accurate. Confederate Secretary Judah P. Benjamin wired from Richmond to Savannah, "The enemy's fleet sailed south this morning; destination unknown." Shortly afterward he was able to predict the target correctly as Port Royal. DuPont took considerable time to get every ship into its proper place in his sailing disposition, but the group finally formed up off Virginia Beach, and headed south toward Cape Hatteras, the "graveyard" of many a fine ship. Unwittingly, DuPont sailed right into the jaws of a hurricane which struck with fury during the night of the thirty-first.

Once again it seemed that nature was on the side of the South. The hurricane ripped apart DuPont's careful formation, wrecked the supply ships *Union* and *Osceola* on the North Carolina coast, broke up the *Peerless* with her load of cattle, and sank the side-wheeler *Governor*. Naval historians recalled how the great storm of the thirteenth century, the "Divine Wind," had saved Japan by destroying a Mongol invading fleet, and gave thanks that DuPont's force had fared better.

It was a combination of Divine Providence and the stubborn determination of Captain Cadwalader Ringgold that saved six hundred marines aboard the hapless *Governor*. In the frigate *Sabine*, Ringgold stood by the *Governor* for eighteen hours during the height of the storm. He anchored his ship nearby and walked out cable until the *Sabine* had drifted down close enough for rescue operations. He passed lines to the *Governor* and rescued about thirty men before the storm increased and parted all but one of the lines. In desperation Ringgold ordered his crew to haul away on the sole connecting hawser, and pulled *Governor* up to *Sabine's* starboard quarter. There about thirty more men jumped to safety on the *Sabine's* decks before Ringgold had to pay out line and let the battered ship drift astern. Somehow the crew of the *Governor* kept her afloat through the night, and in the calmer waters of dawn the *Sabine* rescued the remaining men with small boats. Three hours later the waterlogged *Governor* sank, but her exhausted men on the *Sabine* were too tired to care.

Captain DuPont scanned the horizon on Saturday morning, November 2, and found only one of his ships within visual signaling distance. Relying on the good seamanship of his officers, and their ability to read sealed orders correctly, he proceeded to Port Royal Sound and waited outside the bar. Gradually his force reassembled and anchored near the flagship *Wabash.* By Monday afternoon, November 4, DuPont realized that the navy would have to fight alone. So many small boats had been destroyed by the hurricane, it would be impossible to land General Sherman's troops ashore as planned.

DuPont had guessed that the Confederates would remove all buoys and navigational aids from the channel, and had brought with him some experts from the U.S. Coast Survey aboard the steamer *Vixen.* In one day's work the *Vixen* sounded out and buoyed a channel, permitting any vessel drawing less than eighteen feet to pass through. All of DuPont's ships of lesser draft entered the roadstead before dark on the fourth, and were followed the next day at high tide by the bigger ships.

The then prevailing concept that one land gun equaled five or ten guns aboard ship was so popular in 1861 that many spectators came down from Charleston in a holiday mood to watch their forts sink DuPont's fleet. However, Union navy planners were not foolhardy enough to send a force against a fort unless it had an overwhelming superiority. This was certainly true in August at Hatteras, where Union guns not only outnumbered the Confederates by a ratio of four to one, but also outranged them by hundreds of yards. At Port Royal DuPont had a comfortable superiority in guns and ammunition. While he had a healthy respect for the Confederate's large old land guns, he nevertheless adopted a plan of battle which brought his force in to close quarters with the enemy. In explaining this plan to his captains, DuPont pointed out the advantage that ships would have if they always presented a moving target.

For the attacking amphibious forces, the Port Royal channel was guarded on the port side by Fort Walker on Hiltonhead Island, where one thousand troops manned a battery of sixteen heavy land guns. To the starboard, on the southern tip of St. Helena Island, stood Fort Beauregard with nineteen guns and a garrison of one hundred and fifty guns. Intelligence estimates available to DuPont credited Fort Walker as the stronger of the two defenses, but pointed out that its design made it particularly susceptible to enfilading fire from the north. DuPont decided to concentrate his heaviest fire on Walker, entering the channel midway between the two forts, and by successive turns to port to remain within good position for enfilade fire at Walker's weakest point. His tactics worked so well that Confederate gunners complained afterward that they would no more than find the range than their target was already in another position. The plan required steamships capable of moving under their own power; however, in order to use all available guns, DuPont ordered the *Isaac Smith* to tow the sailing sloop *Vandalia* into the firing line. The *Isaac Smith* had thrown all of her guns overboard to survive the hurricane, but *Vandalia* had not. Needless to say, it was an object lesson to the *Isaac Smith*'s crew, who had to face gunfire without being able to shoot back.

Before DuPont could press his bombardment, he had to dispose of a Confederate "fleet" whose strength lay entirely in its nuisance value. Commanded by Captain Josiah Tattnall, a veteran of thirty years' service in the U.S. Navy, Southern naval forces consisted of one river steamer, two armed tugs, and one small ram. Tattnall's flagship *Savannah* was commanded by none other than John Newland Maffitt, later to become the South's most successful blockade-runner. Unable to pose any real threat to the superior Union force, Tattnall had to take safety in Skull Creek shortly after USS *Seneca* scored a hit on the *Savannah* with an eleven-inch gun.

With Confederate naval opposition out of the way, DuPont ordered his ships to bombard positions promptly at 8:00 A.M. on November 7. Nine heavy ships flanked by five gunboats moved slowly through the channel. At 9:26 the guns from Fort Walker opened fire, and were followed immediately by batteries at Fort Beauregard. One by one the old wooden ships steamed into the Confederate fire, closing to ranges as small as six hundred yards. DuPont wrote his wife after the battle of "rifle balls whizzing over our heads," indicating how dangerously close his ships were at the height of battle. Firing was hot on both sides, but a great deal of it was aimed too high. Some Union shells fell into a cotton field a mile and a half away, but this could happen easily with a flat trajectory that just missed the top of Fort Walker. Likewise, Confederate fire was too high, striking ships' rigging, splintering masts, tearing away halyards, shrouds, and iron stays, but not breaching any hulls.

None of DuPont's ships went unscathed. The *Wabash* suffered many hits from all sides. The *Susquehanna* was hit ten times and the *Pawnee* took four solid hits in her superstructure. Men on both sides fought like demons in the deafening din, stepping over the torn bodies of their comrades to maintain fire. After the battle, a Confederate colonel commented on the damage caused by enfilade fire, observing, "The enemy, having taken position in the mouth of the Creek, exposed us to a raking fire which did us the greatest damage, dismounting our guns, and killing and wounding numbers of our men." Official reports listed thirty-five Union dead and wounded and sixty-six Confederate casualties, but soldiers who occupied the forts counted an additional fifty-two bodies left behind by General Thomas Fenwick Drayton's troops.

The Confederates at Port Royal experienced the same difficulties that Commodore Barron had at Hatteras; ammunition ran so low that they could only maintain a slow token fire. Meanwhile the carnage wrought by the Union bombardment mounted. The *Wabash* alone fired almost nine hundred shells, which in all probability exceeded the entire ammunition supply at Fort Walker. Shortly after 1:00 P.M. General Drayton, faced with a hopelessly deteriorating situation, decided to evacuate. By 2:45 DuPont sensed that the battle was over and gave the order to cease firing. He sent his aide, Commander John Rogers, ashore under a flag of truce. Rogers found a terrible scene of death and destruction amid a mass of scattered arms, legs, and torsos. He ran up the Stars and Stripes and news of the victory circled rapidly through the Union ships.

Troopships in the roads got underway and anchored a few hundred yards off the beach to disembark detachments of soldiers to take permanent possession of the fort. Fort Beauregard was found to be abandoned, and it was occupied by General Sherman's troops on the following morning. The Union garrisons worked feverishly to prepare for an enemy counterattack, but it never came.

News of the victory at Port Royal electrified the North, where rumors exaggerated the action to include surrender of Savannah and burning of Charleston. These feats could have been accomplished easily in the turmoil and confusion that struck throughout South Carolina and Georgia, but Sherman and DuPont refused to press on. The capture of Port Royal was, nevertheless, an important victory for the North, and prompted Congress to pass a joint resolution of thanks to Captain Samuel F. DuPont for his "decisive and splendid victory." After a series of heartbreaking disappointments, the North now had another substantial accomplishment that restored faith in themselves and stiffened their attitude toward the war.

⚓

FIVE

Forts Henry and Donelson

THE "interior" of the United States was assigned exclusively to the Union army for the prosecution of Civil War campaigns. This interior (the Midwest) comprised the fertile agricultural basin of the Mississippi River and its tributaries. It had almost no roads of any length, and very few railroads. As a result, army commanders who wished to move troops and supplies were forced to use the intricate system of rivers which had served this area as highways of commerce since the days of the early French explorers.

Under Jefferson Davis' direction, the Confederacy adopted a perimeter defense of its interior, and set up numerous forts at strategic points on the rivers bordering its heartland. Army commanders, tired of slogging through swamps and forests only to be stopped by these fortifications, soon learned the value of floating artillery. Indeed, it was almost impossible to move heavy guns needed for destruction of Rebel strongholds in any other way.

Once embarked upon a course of action that depended upon rivers for strategic, tactical, and logistic considerations, the army looked to the Union navy for assistance. This led to the establishment of a "freshwater" navy which operated with distinction throughout the war. It received its baptism of fire in February of 1862 against two Confederate forts—Fort Henry on the Tennessee River, and Fort Donelson on the Cumberland River.

The history of the Union freshwater navy is one of many paradoxes. First of all, the ships belonged to the army, but they were designed by naval officers on loan to the War Department. The craft were manned and fought by navy crews under overall direction of army generals. Freshwater action produced the first ironclad a month before the *Monitor* met the *Merrimac*. The river navy can be

[49]

said to have given the North its first general who could win battles consistently. For in a sense, it was General Ulysses S. Grant's understanding of river "sea power" and his tactical use of gunboats in connection with land operations that made him an outstanding success in the Midwest.

The ships of the freshwater navy were built by a young and successful industrialist, James Buchanan Eads of St. Louis. The little gunboats displaced about 512 tons, were 175 feet long, 50 feet wide, and had a draft of 6 feet. The boat's hull supported a completely covered casemate which had sides sloping at forty-five degrees up to a flat roof. The forward part of this covering was fitted with a 2½-inch iron plate as protection for two 10-inch guns. On each side of this upper shell there were openings for four 32-pound guns. Because of their appearance, and in honor of navy constructor Sam Pook, their designer, they were fondly called "Pook's Turtles"! However useful they proved to be, they had many faults. They were miserably slow, hot, their gunports were so poorly designed that high-angle fire was impossible, and their guns were just a few feet above water.

When Flag Officer Andrew H. Foote hoisted his flag over the gunboat squadron in January 1862, he had seven of these "turtles"— *St. Louis, Cairo, Carondelet, Louisville, Cincinnati, Pittsburg*, and *Mound City*. In addition to the Pook boats, Foote had five other wooden gunboats—*Lexington, Tyler, Essex, Benton*, and *Conestoga*. This was a formidable fleet on paper, but Foote and his officers had to work around the clock before they had their crews and ships ready for combat. The anxious Foote, who quickly became a friend of Brigadier General U. S. Grant, wrote to the overall army commander, Major General Henry W. Halleck, that he was ready: "General Grant and myself are of the opinion that Fort Henry, on the Tennessee River, can be carried with four gunboats and troops and be permanently occupied."

Halleck waited for several days, but on January 30 ordered a combined operation up the Tennessee, and warned General Grant that the roads were quagmires. He directed that all army troops, munitions, and supplies be moved in convoy with Foote's gunboats. The objective of this combined army-navy operation was to seize control of the Tennessee and Cumberland rivers and occupy the two Confederate strongholds—Forts Henry and Donelson. The plan called for a joint land-sea attack on Fort Henry first, followed by a quick shift of troops overland to Fort Donelson. Foote's boats would have to move quickly around to the Cumberland so they could assist Grant's attack on the second fort.

Fort Henry was one of those muddy dirt forts which the South threw up hurriedly in the first year of the war. It was located at a bend in the Tennessee River so that its sixteen guns would cover river approaches from either direction. This was an ideal location as far as river coverage was concerned, but unfortunately the terrain was unsuitable, and the fort was frequently threatened with floods. Foote was fortunate that his first gunboat action would be against this low-lying fortification, which was just about on a level with his own ships' guns. Nevertheless, Fort Henry was not an easy target. It was a large post, with facilities to handle six thousand men, but Confederate General Tighlman had only about one third that number on the day that Foote attacked.

The naval force departed from Cairo, Illinois, on February 2, Foote's gunboats in the lead ahead of Grant's fleet of commandeered river ferries. On the fourth, Grant's first echelon of troops landed about five miles below Fort Henry in a waterlogged forest that was almost completely covered with floodwaters. Grant was dissatisfied with this turn of events, so he asked Foote to take him down to reconnoiter the fort from a closer position. The *Essex* ran down within range of Fort Henry's rifle guns and exchanged a few "feeling-out" shots. One shell whistled by General Grant, taking the head off a man standing nearby. This was enough to convince the general that it would be wiser and safer for his troops to attack the fort overland, despite the mud and flooded creeks.

On another occasion Grant was aboard the *Cincinnati* with Foote when the navy commander directed his crew to recover and bring aboard one of the Confederate mines that had broken its moorings. It was placed aft for disassembly and inspection. The two senior officers went to the fantail, by descending a ladder from the gun-deck, and watched the ship's gunner dismantle it. Suddenly there was a sharp "hiss" as some pent-up gas escaped from the strange-looking box. Immediately there was chaos as all hands sought cover, running in every direction with no respect for rank. General Grant beat Foote up the ladder to safety on the gundeck. When the harmless hissing stopped, Foote turned to the general and asked,

"General, why all this haste?"

"To keep the navy from getting ahead of me," Grant replied.

Foote was a perfectionist when he prepared for battle; he gave great attention to even the smallest details. His first battle plan and operation order stressed coolness, precision of fire, and provident use of ammunition. He advised his gunners that each shell fired cost the government eight dollars and pointed out that, "random firing is not merely a waste of ammunition, but what is far worse, it encourages the enemy when he sees shot and shell falling harmlessly about and beyond him."

Having satisfied themselves with the day's reconnaissance, General Grant and Flag Officer Foote decided to attack Fort Henry on the sixth. As they waited through the night before D day, a thunderstorm broke over the river and a pouring rain fell all night long. Confederates in Fort Henry wondered if they would be flooded out before the Yankees came, but hoped that the downpour would also flood the forest and make it impossible for Grant's troops to attack from the rear.

At daylight the rains stopped and Foote got his seven boats ready for the attack. He waited until noon to give Grant's troops time to move through the forest into position, and at 12:36 opened fire from a range of about seventeen hundred yards. A believer in close action, Foote brought his four "turtles" into ranges of six hundred yards or less, where it was almost impossible for either side to miss. Neither the gun crews on the boats, nor those in the forts had any previous experience, but they were determined to keep firing until one or the other had had enough. It was a bitterly contested duel that lasted a little over an hour.

Aboard the flagship *Cincinnati*, Foote himself narrowly missed death as a shot struck the pilothouse a few feet from his head. During the battle the *Cincinnati* received thirty-one hits with one man killed and nine wounded. The *St. Louis* and the *Carondelet* were hit half a dozen times each, but suffered no casualties. It was a different story on the *Essex*. Midway in the fight a shell passed through one of her open ports and exploded the middle boiler. Hot steam and scalding water sprayed about the ship, and the *Essex* dropped out of action with three dead and twenty-nine wounded. Some men were so badly scalded they never saw action again.

Meanwhile, things were not going too well inside Fort Henry. Confederate General Tighlman tried to draw out the fighting, hoping that the delay would permit the majority of his troops to escape to Fort Donelson. His big twenty-four pounder exploded, wounding every man of the gun crew. One by one his lighter pieces went out of action either from enemy fire or from faulty ammunition. One of them exploded and killed two men. After an hour of firing he had lost two thirds of his guns, and water was rising above the waists of men in the lower battery. At 1:55 P.M., well before Grant and his troops arrived through the woods, Tighlman raised the white flag. Shortly thereafter, he came aboard the *Cincinnati* to discuss terms of surrender with Flag Officer Foote, and learned that the terms were "Unconditional."

Foote praised Tighlman for his defense and assured him that he would testify that he had "defended his post like a brave man." He reported to Secretary Welles that Tighlman had gone into action with eleven guns of heavy caliber and had fought until seven of them were useless. The Confederates lost five men killed, five missing, and five wounded. Ten officers and fifty men were made prisoners.

When General Grant arrived the surrender was complete. The army was criticized for letting the majority of Tighlman's force escape overland to Donelson, but those who complained could not have realized the effect of the heavy rains. On the other hand Foote's telegram announcing Fort Henry's surrender was sent to Congress where it was read to both houses. Fox and Welles basked in reflected glory for their little river navy, and were congratulated by the President himself.

Leaving the *Carondelet* as a guard ship at Fort Henry, Foote proceeded quickly to Cairo with three damaged ironclads in order to be ready for the next move on Fort Donelson. He sent Lieutenant Phelps in charge of the *Tyler, Conestoga,* and *Lexington* on a sweep up the Tennessee River. A dashing and capable officer who never received the recognition he deserved, Phelps turned in an admirable performance in his three-day trip, destroying six Confederate steamers, seizing three more, and capturing a variety of useful supplies. He penetrated as far as Florence, Alabama, before turning back to join Foote. His greatest prize was the steamer *Eastport,* which the Confederates had started to equip as an ironclad. Chasing away Rebels bent on scuttling her, Phelps patched up the *Eastport's* sides and towed her back to Cairo where she was completed and fitted out for service with Foote's squadron.

The sudden loss of Fort Henry and Phelp's sweep up the Tennessee so shocked the South that a wave of alarm swept through all Southern river states. General Joseph E. Johnston voiced these feelings in his comments on the action: "The capture of Fort Henry by the enemy gives them control of the navigation of the Tennessee River, and their gunboats are now ascending the river to Florence . . . Should Fort Donelson be taken it will open the route to the enemy to Nashville, giving them the means of breaking the bridges and destroying the ferryboats on the river as far as navigable."

He was correct: Fort Donelson was next on the list. As General Grant moved to complete this last phase of his double-barreled operation, he realized that Fort Donelson would be a more difficult task. Unlike Fort Henry, which had been built almost at water level, Donelson's batteries were mounted on hills near the riverbank in a position that permitted plunging fire into any gunboats that came into range. Moreover, Tighlman's defense at Fort Henry had permitted the majority of his force to reach and reinforce Donelson, which now had a garrison of twenty-one thousand men. Against this formidable force Grant had fifteen thousand men and Foote's river flotilla.

He sent an urgent message to General Halleck, who relayed it to Foote, begging him to act quickly, "even though only half ready." Foote did not hesitate, sailing with three gunboats within two hours after he had received the message. He did this with misgivings, however, and wrote to Secretary Welles that he was leaving with only three boats, but that he could have a fleet of six armored boats and eight mortar boats if he could wait ten more days. To his chagrin he found later that mortar boats were exactly what he needed to silence enemy batteries one hundred feet above his own level on the river.

While Foote was making his way down from Cairo, Grant ordered the *Carondelet* into position to help isolate the fort and to restrict traffic across the river. Commander Henry Walke moved into range of the fort's guns on the thirteenth and conducted a deliberate long-range duel. During the morning he fired one hundred and thirty-nine shells, knocking out a nine-pound gun and damaging the fort's columbiad so that it was almost useless. In return the *Carondelet* received a hit that wounded eleven men, most of them struck by flying wooden splinters. Walke transferred his wounded, fed his men their noon meal, and returned to the unequal engagement for the rest of the afternoon. Under cover of darkness he withdrew downriver and there met an impatient and irritable Foote, who could not understand why gunboat action had been ordered before he had arrived.

Foote called his usual commanding officer's conference during the evening and discussed strategy for the following day. He planned to use the same tactics that had served him so well against Fort Henry—sending in his "turtles" bow on to the fort and closing to very short range, keeping his wooden ships in position behind where they could fire at extreme ranges.

Here again, the weather had a hand in the action. While it had rained heavily at Henry, a quick shift in the wind brought sleet, snow, and chilling cold to Donelson. The morning of the fourteenth dawned bitterly, with two inches of snow on the ground. Troops on both sides suffered heavily in the cold; none had tents or overcoats. In the fighting that followed many wounded men froze to death, bodies stiffening before they drew their last breath.

Foote delayed getting underway until he had a conference with Grant, who came aboard to make sure that his plan for joint action was thoroughly understood. A group of transports had arrived early that morning, bringing ten thousand more troops for Grant's armies. It took some time to unload these men and their supplies, so it was not until 2:00 P.M. that Foote could get his ships underway. He attacked Fort Donelson at three o'clock, leading a force of four iron-clads—*St. Louis, Carondelet, Louisville,* and *Pittsburg* in the van, with the wooden gunboats *Tyler* and *Conestoga* in the rear.

At two thousand yards all ships opened fire, and kept up a continuous barrage as Foote bore in to four hundred yards. His task was to silence the batteries and then push upstream to a position where he could enfilade entrenched Confederate positions as Du-Pont had done at Port Royal. In an hour and a half engagement, the freshwater Union navy met its first defeat. Although they could drive the Confederate gun crews from their batteries, they could not keep them away. These determined gunners would return as soon as the gunboats slackened fire, and would deal out punishing blows of their own with plunging fire that penetrated the boats' iron plating. In one of the most fiercely contested battles of the war, the little gunboats took incredible punishment. The flagship *St. Louis* was hit fifty-nine times, and finally drifted downstream out of action when her steering gear was shot away. Two of the hits wounded Flag Officer Foote, one in the arm, and the second in the ankle. The *Pittsburg* with twenty hits and the *Louisville* with thirty-seven hits also drifted out of action. The remaining boats, all suffering casualties from the plunging fire, soon pulled out and followed their leader to a position of safety downstream. Many of the boats had decks slippery with blood, and unwounded men gasped and retched as they moved about amongst the torn arms, legs, and headless torsos.

During the morning of the fifteenth, Foote's men buried their dead and bandaged their wounded. Emergency repairs made the *Louisville* and the *St. Louis* ready for operations once again.

While the navy rested the armies met in a fierce action that almost ended in defeat for General Grant. On this day, perhaps more than any other, he showed the mettle that was to lead him eventually to victory at Appomattox. Calmly he rallied his troops, returned to the fight, and took time to send off a request to Foote for another show of force against the Confederate defenses. This request was received by Lieutenant Commander Benjamin Dove, commanding officer of the *Louisville,* who had assumed overall command when the wounded Foote departed for Cairo.

Once more the two battered little ships moved into the battle, pounding away at the fort until dark. The deep boom of navy guns was reassuring to Grant's troops giving them, according to General Lew Wallace, "positive pleasure . . . and admiration for the obstinacy and courage of the Commodore." He went on to say that the gunboats created a diversion and distracted the enemy. He was certain that their presence prevented a general Rebel retreat across the river.

Early in the morning on Sunday the sixteenth, Confederate General Simon B. Buckner sent officers to General Grant to arrange surrender terms. When Commander Dove returned to the fort with his ships cleared for action, he saw the white flag of surrender and withdrew.

In the great victory at Donelson, General Grant captured fifteen thousand man and ruined the Confederate outer river defense as General Johnston had feared. There is no doubt that the credit for this victory belonged to the army, but the freshwater navy put Grant into position and assisted him ably in the two-day battle. It should be remembered that the gunboats went into action against the best judgment of their commodore, who answered Grant's urgent plea for help without a moment's hesitation, replying, "I sail within two hours." In order to make a fair estimate of the navy's contribution at Fort Donelson, it is only necessary to ask what would have happened if the gunboats had not been there—or if they had belonged to the other side.

The results at Donelson reached far beyond the capture of General Buckner and his large garrison. Confederates learned the value of hilltop positions for river defense, remembering well the effect of plunging fire on the ironclads. Throughout the Southland, wherever it was possible, river defenses were shifted to higher ground. To avoid the punishing effects of plunging fire, the river navy resorted to longer-range bombardment and the use of high-angle firing mortars. Foote was quick to see this, writing to his wife immediately after Fort Donelson that, "I will not go so near again, although at Fort Henry I produced an effect by it." He went on to voice his misgivings and described the fierce action in these simple words, "We ought to have been victorious at Donelson, as we fought harder than at Henry. I went into it against my judgment by order of Halleck. We had fifty-four killed and wounded, and fifty-nine shots in one vessel—a thing never before heard of in a naval fight."

Perhaps the most telling blow struck by the Confederates in this engagement was one of the shots that wounded Flag Officer Foote. It proved to be a mortal wound which brought death to this determined and brave leader after a year's illness.

⚓

SIX

The *Monitor* and the *Merrimac*

THE battle between the little *Monitor* and the cumbersome *Merri-mac,* the most famous naval action of the Civil War, was a great drama of two acts. Time has almost rung down the curtain of oblivion on the first act, the engagement of March 8. There the *Merrimac* nearly fulfilled the South's fond dream of sinking the Union navy with one impregnable vessel. Not only was this duel between the wooden and iron ships one of the most significant engagements in naval history, it was also about the largest fleet action of the entire Civil War.

The second act began on a quiet Sunday morning, March 9, when the *Monitor* completed a race with time and emerged from the drawing board to the role of defender of Hampton Roads in five short months. It was a feat of engineering and forced-draft development unheralded in naval annals, and is rivaled today only with the fantastic accomplishments of ship builders during World War II. The players in both acts of this Civil War drama were some of the bravest men who ever went to sea.

Ironclads were first built by the French in 1854, for use against Russian forts at Kinburn on the shore of the Black Sea. The first attempt produced a flat-bottom boat, with iron-plated sides that had openings for the ship's guns. These craft proved to be so heavy that it was impractical to put engines in them, so they became "floating batteries." They were towed from France to the Black Sea, where their iron-protected sides withstood Russian fire and their guns slowly reduced the forts to ruins.

After this practical demonstration, the world knew that there would be great advantages for the ironclad in the future—as soon as one could be designed with an efficient engineering plant. The French and British navies immediately began an arms race to develop seagoing ironclads. The French armored ship *Gloire* was launched in 1859, and by the time the Civil War began, France had a total of seven armored frigates and England four.

Confederate Navy Secretary Mallory knew that it would be hopeless for the agricultural South to attempt to build a navy that could challenge the Union on the high seas. Influenced by the great claims for ironclads, as well as the success of the French at Kinburn, he sent agents abroad to purchase an ironclad for the Confederacy. Perhaps he could not build a navy to challenge the Union, but possibly if he could obtain one of the armored monsters from the French or British he could sweep the Union navy from the seas. His agents reported that neither the British nor French would sell; each country had its own problems trying to keep up with the other. If the Confederates wanted such a ship they would have to build it themselves. Mallory did not give up. The ironclad was his only hope, and the only practical means of breaking the Union blockade that drew tighter about the South each day. He appointed a board of officers to draw up plans for an armored ship.

These stubborn officers set about their task knowing that they did not have shipyards or factories capable of building such a ship. But they did have the remains of one of the finest frigates in the Union navy lying in the mud at Norfolk Navy Yard, and that yard had one of the best dry docks in the world. Why not, argued the board, raise the hulk and see if it could be salvaged? Accordingly, the *Merrimac* was raised from her watery grave, put into the Norfolk dry dock, pumped out and cleaned. Lieutenants John M. Brooke and John L. Porter of Secretary Mallory's board inspected her and found the frame in excellent condition, and the engines still salvagable. They decided to use the hull as a foundation for their ironclad, covering the old berth deck with four-inch armor plate. Fifteen hundred men went to work on remodeling the *Merrimac*, as Secretary Mallory spurred them on and spared no expense in this one great effort. In late February 1862, Southerners launched the *Merrimac* from her berth in dry dock and renamed her the *Virginia*. In spite of this rechristening, she is remembered to history as the *Merri-mac.*

Lincoln's spy system kept Washington officials informed of the *Merrimac's* progress, and in spite of the South's deliberate efforts to play down hopes for their ironclad, the spy ring continued to pour in alarming news. One report credited the *Merrimac* with a sharp bow and stern, angled sloping superstructure, two engines of great power, and twenty guns. It was even reported that she was fitted with a number of pipes for throwing hot water. Another spy reported that Norfolk newspapers called the ship a failure. As Mallory's pet project progressed, however, it soon became evident that the *Merri-mac* was a dangerous threat and that something had to be done about it—soon. The South had a three-month advantage.

Secretary Welles already had an ironclad board which had been authorized by Congress in August 1861, and one and a half million dollars had been appropriated for the construction of ironclads. Welles' board members decided that it would be best to concentrate on ships of light draft, as they envisioned Union ironclads operating in shallow ocean waters and in Southern rivers. From over one hundred designs the board sifted out two that looked promising. The first one was designed by Merrick and Sons of Philadelphia— the *New Ironsides.* Armed with 4½-inch iron plate, and carrying sixteen 11-inch Dahlgren guns, *New Ironsides* became one of the most powerful "clads" of the war, and later saw action in the siege of Charleston. Unfortunately she was not far enough along with her construction to help Secretary Welles with his immediate problem of containing the *Merrimac* in Hampton Roads.

Northern hopes soon fell upon the shoulders of an eccentric who had no use for the Union navy—John Ericsson, a Swedish inventor who came to America in the 1840's. Disappointed in an earlier experience with naval authorities, Ericsson refused to submit a bid to the Navy Department, but instead sent a copy of his plans for an ironclad direct to President Lincoln. This led to meetings with the ironclad board who were skeptical from the beginning and demanded that the inventor demonstrate first that his model would float.

[61]

Ericsson finally convinced everyone that not only could he build an ironclad that would float, but also that he could do it in one hundred days. The hull was built at Greenpoint, Long Island, by the Continental Ironworks. Subcontractors produced the engine, turret, and armor plate.

As various parts were fitted into place, it became apparent that "Ericsson's Folly" was a strange new craft of radical design. It was 124 feet long, 18 feet wide in the lower hull, but its sloping sides increased the width to 34½ feet in the middle of the ship, where the lower hull was attached to a large wooden raft. The raft was pointed at both ends and measured 172 feet by 41½ feet. The lower hull was below the waterline; it housed boilers, magazines, living quarters, and turret machinery—all protected behind half-inch iron. The wooden raft was covered with one-inch iron plate, except for the center where a large brass ring supported the ship's lone turret. This turret was an innovation. It was a cylinder 9 feet high and 20 feet across, heavily plated with eight-inch armor, and pierced with gunports for two 11-inch Dahlgren guns. The whole turret revolved on a metal spindle that was turned by a steam engine in the bottom of the ship. To provide clearance for gun firing in all directions, Ericsson did not mount a smokestack on his ship, and provided only a small conning tower forward beneath the turret's line of fire. Smoke escaped through a small deck-level grating. Fresh air for the crew was drawn in through similar gratings, and stale air ventilated through hatches in the top of the turret. The inventor installed two steam-driven fans to circulate air.

There were over forty brand-new developments in Ericsson's ship, all of which were eventually patented in his name. Some of them, such as his turret and ammunition elevator, have been copied in naval construction for about one hundred years. The designs for over three thousand mechanical parts needed for the *Monitor* were completed at the inventor's drawing board and then sent directly to the factory or foundry for construction. As work progressed, Ericsson often had to modify his plans on the spot. For example, the contract called for masts, sails, and rigging to propel the ship at six knots in a fair breeze. There wasn't enough room in the ship's hull for storage, so Ericsson ignored the sailing requirement.

Secretary Welles had suggested that the new ironclad be named the *Ericsson* in honor of its inventor, but John Ericsson demurred in favor of the *Monitor*, believing this name to be more symbolic. He felt that his *Monitor* would admonish not only the wayward South for secession, but also it would serve as a threat to the British, who had been rather difficult to get along with after the *Trent* affair.

On January 30, the *Monitor* slid down the ways and floated proudly before a wildly cheering crowd. Among the spectators was a Southern sympathizer who hurried home after the launching to make sketches which eventually found their way to Confederate officers building the *Merrimac*. On the strength of these, the *Merrimac*'s builders lengthened their ironclad's ram so that it could reach the *Monitor*'s underwater hull. This modification weakened the ram to such an extent that it broke after the *Merrimac* struck the *Cumberland,* causing a leak that plagued the ship later when she fought her famous duel with the *Monitor*.

The *Merrimac*'s crew moved aboard on February 17. All were volunteers, and strangely enough many came from the army camps around Richmond and Yorktown. About one week later, on the twenty-fifth, Lieutenant John L. Worden took command of the *Monitor* with a crew of ten officers and forty-five crewmen—all volunteers, too.

Worden took the *Monitor* to sea for trials which went so badly that the little ship had to be towed back to the harbor. Ericsson went through the ship in a frenzy, fixing the faulty main engine valves, instructing the *Monitor*'s gun crew how to use his invention for stopping gun recoil, and designing a block and tackle for moving her sluggish rudder. Everything worked well on the second trial, so Worden headed for Hampton Roads on March 6, in accordance with orders given to him by Commodore Paulding, commandant of the New York Navy Yard. Fortunately another message from Secretary Welles ordering the *Monitor* to Washington was delayed in transit and never got through.

[63]

Leaving New York in good weather, the *Monitor* was taken in tow by her accompanying tug to make better speed. But around noon the next day a storm swept in from the outer reaches of the broad Atlantic, threatening to plunge the little *Monitor* to the bottom. Seas broke over the ship and water poured in through the smoke and air gratings, almost putting out boiler fires and cutting off ventilation. Her sailors had to bail water throughout the night using a human chain to pass buckets up to the turret hatch. Just before daylight the *Monitor* entered smooth seas again, and none too soon. Worden and his men were nearly exhausted from their battle with the storm. At 4:00 P.M. on March 8, when the *Monitor* rounded Cape Henry, Worden heard the sound of booming cannons up ahead at Hampton Roads, but the sluggish ship did not arrive until well after dark. She drew alongside the *Roanoke* at 9:00 P.M. so that Worden could go aboard to report to Captain John Marston, senior officer present.

The roar of cannons that could be heard at Hampton Roads that Saturday afternoon was the death knell for old wooden ships. Worden was listening to the Union navy's frantic effort to stop the impregnable *Merrimac*. Under command of Captain Franklin Buchanan, formerly commanding officer of the Washington Navy Yard, but now with the Confederate navy, the *Merrimac* had been delayed by bad weather on March 7, but had swept into Hampton Roads on Saturday, the eighth, to terrorize the Union fleet.

Six months before it would have been suicide for a single ship to challenge the entire Union blockading force in Hampton Roads. It was even worse for an untried ship whose guns had never been fired, whose crew were strangers to one another, and whose commanding officer has risen from a sick bed to go to sea. This was the *Merrimac*, the "failure" that steamed at barely five knots and turned with great difficulty. Not only did it steam right into the jaws of the Union naval force, but it also withstood supporting fire from Fort Monroe and other army shore batteries. Opposing the *Merrimac*, and first in her path, were the sailing sloop *Cumberland* with twenty-two 9-inch Dahlgrens and one 10-inch pivot gun, and the sailing frigate *Congress* with eight 10-inch Dahlgrens and forty 32-

pound guns. Out by Fort Monroe were the steam frigates *Minnesota* and *Roanoke,* sister ships of the *Monitor,* carrying between them twelve hundred men and over eighty 9-inch and 11-inch guns. In addition, there was the sailing frigate *St. Lawrence,* which survived the two-day battle by going aground in shallow water beyond the reach of *Merrimac's* guns. The three sailing ships mounted a total of one hundred and twenty-four guns and carried crews totaling one thousand men.

Against this fleet, the *Merrimac* had a crew of three hundred and fifty officers and men to run her engineering plant and operate her ten guns—one 7-inch Brooke rifle at each end on a pivot, and eight guns in the armored casemates, four to each side. Accompanying the *Merrimac* on the first day were five other small ships that fought bravely and gave good accounts of themselves. Steaming with her out of the Elizabeth River were the gunboats *Beaufort* and *Raleigh;* and joining her in Hampton Roads was the Richmond flotilla consisting of the *Patrick Henry, Teaser,* and *Jamestown,* under Commander John R. Tucker. This latter group had been outfitted in Richmond and had come down the James River to a point about ten miles above Newport News, where Tucker waited for word that the *Merrimac* was actually coming out to fight. Tucker got underway and fought his way past Union-held shore batteries in time to take *Congress* under fire and support the Confederate ironclad throughout the day.

Buchanan had gotten the *Merrimac* underway from the Norfolk Yard early in the morning, with mechanics still aboard. He disembarked these at Craney Island and took the *Merrimac* on her first day's trial and first day's battle simultaneously. She was so slow and sluggish that it was necessary for the *Beaufort* to pass a line from ahead to keep her steady on course down the channel. At about 1:00 P.M. Buchanan's little group entered the James River and headed for the two nearest ships, the *Congress* and the *Cumberland,* who were taking it easy on a quiet Saturday afternoon and had their crew's washed clothes on the line.

The well-drilled crews of these old sailing ships manned their batteries quickly and were ready and waiting before the *Merrimac*

[65]

closed the range. At 2:00 P.M. the *Beaufort* fired the first shot at the *Congress* who ignored this little ship and blasted solid shot at the *Merrimac* from her stern gun. When the shot struck the *Merrimac's* casemate, it glanced off like water off a duck's back. The Confederate replied with a charge of grape into the *Congress'* wooden sides, killing several men. This set the day's pattern. Union sailors stuck bravely to their guns despite heavy casualties and poured shot after shot into the *Merrimac* with little apparent damage.

Buchanan had informed his officers that he would ram Union vessels whenever he could in order to conserve his scarce supply of ammunition. He chose the *Cumberland,* whose rifled guns were the greatest threat to the *Merrimac's* four-inch armor plate. Sweeping by the *Congress* and leaving his two little escorts, the *Beaufort* and the *Raleigh,* to keep her occupied, the *Merrimac* headed straight for the towering *Cumberland,* receiving heavy broadsides as she approached. Buchanan shouted across the water for his opponent to surrender, but received a stout "Never," in reply. It would have been better for both ships if they had come to terms. A few minutes later the *Cumberland* was holed and sinking with over one third of her crew dead or wounded, but before she went down, she inflicted more damage than the Confederate ironclad would receive from all the rest of the Union ships, including the *Monitor* on the following day.

In the last hundred yards before the *Merrimac* rammed her, the *Cumberland* scored two bull's-eyes right through the Confederate's casemate portal, killing or wounding seventeen men. But the ironclad kept coming, and crashed into the sailing ship just forward of her fore channels. The *Cumberland* staggered and began to settle quickly, but her crew kept cheering and firing. They shot away the muzzles of two of the *Merrimac's* guns and snapped her anchor chain. The shattered chain slashed back into the ship, killing two and wounding five more. Soon it was all over; the *Cumberland* sank to the bottom and turned over on her side, taking with her the ironclad's metal ram, which broke off when Buchanan backed away.

Buchanan now turned his attention to the *Congress,* determined to sink her even though his own brother was aboard as acting paymaster. Young Captain Joseph B. Smith on the *Congress* had learned enough from the *Cumberland's* experience to know what to expect if the heavy ironclad rammed his wooden sides. He slipped his cable and steered the *Congress* into a mud bank near friendly land batteries. There he found himself under the concentrated fire of five little gunboats, including Commander Tucker's Richmond flotilla, which had joined the battle to keep the *Congress* busy while Buchanan maneuvered for a new attack. The forts along the James River harassed the *Merrimac* as she turned toward the grounded Union vessel. Their fire was so annoying that Buchanan returned it, silencing several guns, sinking a schooner, and blowing up a large transport.

Soon he was in a position to finish off the *Congress,* pouring in broadside after broadside until her decks ran with blood. Then came one of the most bitterly argued events of the war. The *Congress* lowered her colors and ran up a white flag, which apparently was not seen throughout the ship. The *Beaufort* and two other gunboats went alongside to take off the wounded but were driven off by heavy artillery and musket fire from shore. Unable to sink the Union ship in her beached position, Buchanan decided to burn her, and ordered Commander Tucker in the *Patrick Henry* to close in and do the job.

The little *Patrick Henry* bored right in, but was taken under fire by guns from Fort Monroe, artillery along the beach, and strangely enough from the *Congress,* even though her white flag showed plainly at the mainmast. In a short while the little gunboat was disabled and had to be towed to safety. When Buchanan saw this, he sent some of the *Merrimac's* crew over in small boats covered by the *Teaser.* The small boats were driven off by rifle fire from the *Congress* in an act that Buchanan called "vile treachery." Accordingly, having lost many good men in his efforts to save additional slaughter, Buchanan ordered the *Merrimac* to resume firing, this time with heated shot. Just before he issued the order, he was struck in the thigh by a rifle ball from shore, and had to turn over command to Lieutenant Catesby ap Roger Jones.

Burning with anger over the Confederate casualties suffered

[67]

under a flag of truce, Catesby Jones resumed fire, using red-hot shells that had been heated in the *Merrimac*'s furnaces. Many of the Federal wounded were hit a second time, and the casualties on the *Beaufort* and the other gunboats increased. Almost hit by Union fire were Lieutenant Pendergrast and Commander William Smith, USN, who had surrendered the *Congress* to Lieutenant Parker of the *Beaufort* an hour earlier, and were now prisoners aboard the gunboat. Soon the hot shells took their toll, and the *Congress* began to burn in several places. With darkness coming on and an ebb tide reducing the *Merrimac*'s margin of safety for maneuvering, Catesby Jones decided to call it a day, and steered for anchorage at Sewell Point, remarking to his officers that the *Merrimac* would return the next day to finish off the *Minnesota* and the rest of the Union fleet. Box score for the day's work accounted for two Union ships and four hundred casualties, against the slightly damaged ironclad with her twenty-one killed or wounded. Confederate losses on the gunboats were: fourteen on the *Patrick Henry*, eight aboard the *Beaufort*, and seven on the *Raleigh*. Spectators along the Confederate shore cheered as the slow ironclad limped to a safe anchorage near Craney Point. At a little after midnight, the fires aboard the *Congress* reached her magazine, causing an explosion that sent flames roaring skyward, and sending her to the bottom of Hampton Roads.

The Confederacy rejoiced and the North was chilled with fear when news of the day's battle spread through the country. Southerners boasted that the *Merrimac* would sweep the Union fleet clear of Hampton Roads in another day, and then would demolish all main Northern seaports one by one. Back in Washington on Sunday morning, President Lincoln called an emergency cabinet meeting, and was annoyed with Secretary of War Stanton, who kept glancing out of the window of the White House to see if the *Merrimac* had arrived yet. The frightened Stanton said, "Not unlikely, we shall have a shell or a cannonball from one of her guns in the White House before we leave this room."

As news of the battle spread, both sides took justifiable pride in the bravery and devotion of the men who manned the ships in that memorable engagement. It took raw courage to stand and fight an iron monster from a wooden ship, but the crews of the *Cumberland* and the *Congress* never flinched. On the other hand, only a brave man would serve aboard a metal coffin like the *Merrimac,* which everyone expected to sink in the first ripple on Hampton Roads. The attitude and feeling prevailing at the time can be best explained by a remark made by old Commodore Smith in Washington when he heard that the *Congress,* his son's ship, had surrendered. "Then Joe's dead," he exclaimed, knowing that his son would never haul down his flag. He was correct.

When darkness rang down the curtain on the first act of the sea drama of Hampton Roads, the other principal actor arrived. Exhausted from thirty-six hours without sleep in the high winds and seas during the voyage down, Lieutenant Worden and his men looked forward to some sleep and rest when they pulled alongside the *Roanoke* that night. Instead they were sent to help the *Minnesota,* aground on a shoal near Newport News and helpless against the *Merrimac* if it returned. When Worden finished conferring with the *Minnesota*'s commanding officer and had anchored the *Monitor* nearby, it was about 3:00 A.M. However, neither he nor his men got much sleep. Catesby Jones got the *Merrimac* underway again at 6:00 A.M. and headed back to Hampton Roads. Jones planned to finish off the *Minnesota* first, and then sink all wooden ships that dared remain in Hampton Roads. In his pocket he carried Secretary Mallory's secret instructions to Captain Buchanan, which directed him to break the blockade and then proceed to New York to demand its surrender.

As the *Merrimac* closed range on the grounded *Minnesota,* sightseers from Norfolk lined the Confederate shores, having come from miles away to witness the slaughter of the Union blockading force. Across the bay near Newport News, Federal troops cheered when the little *Monitor* pulled away from the *Minnesota* and moved between her and the Confederate ironclad. Officers on the *Merrimac* were surprised to see this strange-looking craft, but so impressed were they with their great success of the day before that they were confident of breaking the blockade and chasing away all Union ships.

The two ironclads opened fire at beginning ranges of about one mile, but closed to less than one hundred yards during most of the fight. Worden had decided in advance that he would capitalize on the *Monitor's* greater maneuverability, and would move around in circles large enough to permit his gun crew to reload. His turret crew was under command of Lieutenant Samuel Dana Greene, who was assisted by First Master Stodder and Chief Engineer Stimers. Each of the eleven-inch Dahlgrens was manned by a crew of eight men, most of whom wondered how the iron-protected turret would stand up under fire. Worden was in the tiny pilothouse, which was barely large enough to hold him; his pilot, Acting Master Howard, and Quartermaster Peter Williams were at the helm. The men aboard the *Monitor* had had little or no sleep during the past two days, and were almost exhausted from constant work and little food. Lieutenant Greene had been awake and on his feet for almost fifty-one hours. The situation was about the same aboard the *Merrimac;* her crew had been up all night repairing leaks and replenishing ammunition. Nevertheless, as soon as the fighting began the tired crews of both ships forgot their fatigue and fought as hard as they could.

The *Merrimac* poured broadside after broadside into the *Monitor* with no apparent effect, and received in return a slow, steady fire from the *Monitor's* revolving turret. Men on both ships learned to trust their ship's armor plating, and only those who leaned against the shields received any injury. Several men aboard the *Merrimac* were bowled over by concussion from the heavy shells that banged the casement shield, and three men were knocked unconscious in the *Monitor's* turret. Worden tried but could not increase the rate of fire. His speaking tubes were shot away, so he had to pass orders to Greene by word of mouth through two messengers. Greene would ask his captain the effect of each shot, but this just added to the confusion. He and his gun crew were almost deafened by the *Merrimac's* broadsides and the noise from their own guns.

Early in the battle, the two ships passed each other on opposite headings. When the *Merrimac* turned around to reengage the *Monitor,* she was quite close to the *Minnesota.* Captain Henry Van

[70]

Brunt delivered a broadside that would have demolished any wooden ship afloat, and he swore that at least fifty solid shot from the *Minnesota* struck the ironclad's slanting sides with no effect.

The *Merrimac* now attempted, without success, to ram the *Monitor,* and she in turn tried to ram the Confederate. Neither attempt was satisfactory, and all the *Merrimac* accomplished by glancing off the *Monitor*'s side armor was to start a leak in her own hull. After two hours of fighting, the *Monitor* hauled off into shallow water to replenish ammunition in her upper turret. In order to pass more powder up from the magazine, a passing hole in the turret floor had to be aligned over a scuttle in the deck below. After about fifteen minutes she was ready to resume fighting and returned in time to distract the *Merrimac* from finishing off the *Minnesota,* which was maintaining a furious fire in desperate defense. Van Brunt was so certain of defeat that he made preparations to blow up his ship rather than surrender her.

Next came one of those moments dreaded by every captain who takes a ship into shoal water—the *Merrimac* went aground. Worden brought his ship adjacent to the grounded Confederate and actually placed his bow against the *Merrimac*'s quarter. From that position Greene fired both eleven-inch guns at point-blank range into the stern of the *Merrimac*'s armored casement. The impact of the shot ripped off some plating and forced the sloping side in about three inches. The crew of the pivot gun fell to the deck, bleeding from nose and ears. If these shots had been fired by a full charge of powder, they would have penetrated the armor plate. Lieutenant Worden had tried to obtain permission to increase the standard powder charge of fifteen pounds, but he had been unsuccessful. Later it was proved that his guns could fire a forty-five pound charge with safety.

When the *Monitor* was in position alongside, Lieutenant Catesby Jones called "away boarders." Just how his boarding party was supposed to get through the *Monitor*'s armored hatches has not been explained, but they could have done some damage. For example, the Confederates thought of several schemes: they could hammer wedges into the roller ring of the *Monitor*'s turret, or drop explosives down the smoke and air gratings, or cover Worden's pilothouse with canvas. However, before the boarders could swarm through the *Merrimac*'s ports, the *Monitor* backed clear.

The *Merrimac* strained to get off the shoal. Finally Chief Engineer Ramsey tied down his safety valves and threw wood and turpentine on the furnace fires to get more steam pressure. The boilers shuddered and the propeller churned up mud. Slowly the heavy ironclad moved clear of the shoal and resumed the fight.

By now both Worden and Catesby Jones had a healthy respect for each other. They had fought to a standstill and had proved that the armored sides of each ship were superior to the guns. At about the same moment each captain decided once again to ram his opponent. The lumbering *Merrimac* missed, and the *Monitor* came slashing in, hoping to smash off the Confederate's propeller, but missed by inches. As she went by, the crew on the *Merrimac*'s stern pivot guns fired at the *Monitor*'s pilothouse from a range of about ten yards. One solid shot struck it squarely, catching Worden peering through the slit and peppered his face with cement. The *Monitor*'s commander was blinded temporarily, and suffered a mild concussion. He sent for Lieutenant Samuel Dana Greene, and took his ship into shallow water until the situation cleared. Greene helped his commander to a sofa in the wardroom before he took charge in the damaged pilothouse. About twenty minutes elapsed before he steered the *Monitor* back into deep water to renew the engagement, but he found that the *Merrimac* had retired, thinking that the fight was over.

Catesby Jones, acting skipper of the *Merrimac*, loved a good fight and was destined to die fighting later in the war. However, his pilot refused to take the *Merrimac* closer to the *Minnesota* for fear of grounding again. Jones called Chief Engineer Ramsey to discuss the situation, stating that he intended to drop back to Sewell Point and wait for high tide before he went after the *Minnesota* again. Ramsey and the other *Merrimac* officers finally persuaded Jones that he should call it a day. The *Merrimac* needed more solid shot, a new ram, and replacements for her damaged guns before resuming the fight. So the Confederate ironclad withdrew just as the *Monitor* was returning to have another go. In this manner the historic battle was ended with each side claiming victory. The judgment of one hundred years of history has been that the contest was a draw.

If the two ships were judged in terms of accomplishment of their assigned mission, the nod would have to go in favor of *Monitor*. She was there to save the *Minnesota,* while the *Merrimac* was there to sink the *Minnesota* and destroy as many other Union ships as possible. The *Merrimac* failed in her mission; the *Monitor* did not. In fact, the *Minnesota* was pulled off the shoal that night and was moved to safety near Fort Monroe.

Neither ship survived long after this first meeting. In the two-month stalemate that followed, the *Monitor* stayed close by to guard other Union blockaders. These ships, a bit more cautious now, lay outside Hampton Roads with steam up at all times. When Norfolk was evacuated by the Confederates on May 10, the *Merrimac's* position was hopeless. Her new commanding officer, Commodore Josiah Tattnall, lightened her to try for a dash up the James River, but his pilots refused to try it in view of an unfavorable wind. There was nothing left but to destroy the ship, and this was done on May 11.

The *Monitor* survived and operated in Virginia rivers and in the Chesapeake until December. On December 31, she was at sea again, en route to Beaufort, when she encountered a gale that sent her to the bottom with all hands aboard.

To each of these ships and their valiant men, the United States owes tribute and an honored place in history. Regardless of the flag they supported, they fought well in the face of tremendous obstacles and fear of the unknown. The ingenuity and invention, born of desperation, that characterized these first ironclads brought about the reconstruction of the navies of the world.

The battle was a draw, with honor enough for both sides.

⚓

SEVEN

The Fall of New Orleans

FABULOUS New Orleans, largest and richest city of the South, was the economic heart of the Confederacy and its most important gateway for trade. In Washington, President Lincoln and his generals dreamed of capturing New Orleans, but the dream always ended in masses of troops inching their way down the Mississippi River with heavy casualties.

There were dreamers in the navy, too—men of vision like Commander David Dixon Porter and Assistant Secretary of the Navy Gus Fox, who could see beyond the difficulties that baffled the Union navy's blockade board. In August 1861 this board investigated their futile efforts to shut off trade to New Orleans, and concluded with the pessimistic statement that "the blockade of the river does not necessarily close the trade of the port." This was true, for New Orleans' traders had a great choice of outlets through the bayous, lakes, and bays that dotted the Gulf tidewater. Gus Fox believed that the only effective way to stop trade in that thriving port was to capture it, but he did not have an acceptable plan. However, Porter, an old hand in Mississippi country who had run a steam packet on the river before the war, did have a plan. The trouble was no one would listen to him.

The mighty Mississippi River, main artery of commerce for the Crescent City, pumped strength and vast wealth into the South; and now, in wartime, it served as a highway for movement of military supplies to Confederate armies. Yet this highway was also open to two-way traffic; Union forces could move on it as well as Confederate. The Federals could attack the city from two directions—Grant's armies from the North, or Welles' ships from the South. However, in 1862 the residents of New Orleans felt reasonably safe

[74]

behind their defenses, and were specially proud of Forts Jackson and Saint Philip ninety miles downstream. The popular feeling at the time was that the city's southern flank was well defended and that the greater danger lay to the north.

Actually the southern approach was the more difficult. Swift river currents made passage by large ships extremely slow, and masonry forts guarded the first big bend in the river from commanding positions. Major General Mansfield Lovell, Confederate commander of New Orleans' defenses, did not have to depend entirely on the firepower of his two forts. He also had a fleet of warships and he had constructed a number of fire rafts to use against an approaching enemy fleet. His last and most formidable defense was a barrier of heavy chains drawn across the river near the two forts. The chains were supported by hulks moored to the river bottom.

After DuPont had demonstrated at Port Royal that wooden steamships could conquer land forts, Assistant Secretary Gus Fox suggested to Secretary Welles and other government officials that the Union navy fight past Forts Saint Philip and Jackson, and proceed on upriver to capture New Orleans. The cautious General George B. McClellan estimated that it would take fifty thousand troops to capture the forts and persuaded President Lincoln that the idea was impractical. Thus Fox's proposal was effectively stalemated until one of the most colorful and energetic officers in naval history arrived in Washington with a headful of ideas about seizing New Orleans.

This was Commander David Dixon Porter, son of a famous naval officer and destined to become a naval immortal in his own right. "Black Dave" Porter was a striking man with a bushy black beard and a persuasive tongue. First he told Fox and Welles of his plan, next the President, and then General McClellan. The key element of Porter's strategy was a brand-new idea—a flotilla of mortar boats mounting thirteen-inch army siege guns. He wanted to mount these heavy guns on dismasted schooners and anchor them below the forts at the river bend. There he would pound the defenses with a heavy barrage, ceasing fire just before a force of seagoing warships dashed past the forts. His idea appealed to the army, because it reduced

[75]

troop requirements to just enough for occupation of the city under protection of fleet guns. Porter convinced General McClellan that only ten thousand men would be needed, and argued that the attack on New Orleans would divert Confederate forces operating in Virginia.

When General McClellan agreed to the overall plan and promised ten thousand army troops, Gideon Welles advocated complete secrecy. They did not tell the War Department or Secretary of War Simon Cameron, and even waited some time before informing Major General Benjamin F. Butler, who was to command the troops assigned to the expedition. Secretary Welles knew that the attack on New Orleans would have a lasting effect on the war, and considered it most important to select the right men to lead the campaign.

Actually Welles had little use for Commander Porter and in fact disliked him personally. He remembered how Porter had snatched the *Powhatan* away from the Fort Sumter expedition, and did not trust him. However, after watching the commander handle himself in conferences with the President and other high officials in Washington, Welles was impressed. To the Secretary's credit, he put aside his personal feelings and appointed young Porter to command the mortar flotilla.

His next and more important task was to select a commander in chief for the expedition. His more familiar officers, the bureau chiefs and blockade commanders, were too busy elsewhere. Captain Stringham, victor at Cape Hatteras, was too old. Welles looked over the list of captains and for the first time considered those of Southern birth. He had been impressed by David Glasgow Farragut, number fifty-seven on the list, when that officer had promptly moved his family from Norfolk at the outbreak of the war. He asked other naval officers for their opinion of this relatively unknown captain whose most notable achievements included establishment of the navy yard at Mare Island, California, and a reputation as a good fleet gunnery officer. The replies were noncommittal; most of the officers respected Farragut, but doubted his ability to lead a large expedition. Porter and Gus Fox recommended him, however, so Welles gave Farragut the command.

Farragut, who was as excited as a young midshipman over the prospects of command and sea duty, wrote to his wife about the good news: "Keep your lips closed, and burn my letters; for perfect silence is to be observed—the first injunction of the Secretary. I am to have a flag in the Gulf, and the rest depends on myself. Keep calm and silent. I shall sail in three weeks."

Official Union navy orders dated January 20 directed Farragut to proceed to the Gulf of Mexico, where he would meet a fleet of mortar schooners and armed steamers under the command of David Porter. Together they were to proceed up the Mississippi River and "reduce the defenses which guard the approaches to New Orleans, when you will appear off that city and take possession of it under the guns of your squadron."

The three elements of the attack force sailed separately: Farragut departed from Hampton Roads on February 2, with forty-seven ships; Porter sailed in the *Harriet Lane* on February 11, with twenty-one mortar schooners under tow; and General Butler left on February 23. Butler's force got away with difficulty due to misunderstandings with General McClellan.

On February 20 Farragut arrived at Ship Island where he joined forces with Flag Officer McKean, commander of the Gulf Coast Blockade Squadron. Flat, sandy Ship Island lay fifteen miles off the Mississippi coast and about sixty-five miles east of New Orleans. Union forces had seized it several months earlier as a base for the Gulf Blockade Squadron, and Farragut found it an admirable staging base for his New Orleans forces. Soon the anchorage at Ship Island was filled with ships, and General Butler's troops swarmed ashore for drill. As a diversionary tactic, Farragut spread the rumor that he was there for an attack on either Mobile or Galveston.

After several weeks of attending to administrative detail and setting up a force to continue the blockade in his absence, Farragut was ready to push upriver. At the mouth of the Mississippi he found the main channels shallow with silt, and had to spend three weeks getting his larger ships over the mud bar. The frigate *Colorado* had too much draft and could not make it even after removal of all guns, personnel, and stores. As a last resort, Farragut assigned the *Colo-*

rado's skipper, Captain Theodorus Bailey, to command the First Gunboat Division and put the ships' guns and gun crews aboard smaller ships.

The difficulties would have discouraged a less determined man than Farragut. It took eleven days to get the *Mississippi* over the bar, and fourteen days for the *Pensacola*. Once inside the river mouth, Farragut had to spend more time reloading guns and stores, and stripping his ships for action. He landed all unnecessary spars, canvas, and loose gear at Pilot Town, and issued instructions to minimize damage from the guns of Forts Saint Philip and Jackson.

On April 16, he moved to a position just below the forts, with a force of 17 warships carrying 154 guns to combat the combined Confederate defenses. Confederate General Lovell had a formidable force which, if properly supplied and directed, might well have defeated Farragut. Fort Jackson, on the western bank of the river, had 58 guns, and Fort Saint Philip had 42 mounted. The Confederate naval forces had 39 guns, a ram, and a version of an ironclad.

Shortly after he arrived in New Orleans, Lovell was surprised to find that naval forces on the river were under two commands and that almost all the fit army troops had been sent north to Virginia and Tennessee. Nevertheless, the forts were in a commanding position at the first turn of the river, and they could concentrate their entire firepower on Farragut's ships as they arrived one by one.

Commander Porter got a chance to use his mortar squadron on April 18. Led by the *Harriet Lane*, the steamers *Clifton* and *Westfield* moved up the river with mortar schooners in tow. Porter's idea was a good one. His mortar ships were about 110 feet long, 28 feet wide, and drew 10 feet. They were much bigger and deeper than the flat-bottom mortar boats used by the army in river warfare. Army experience had been disappointing. High-angle fire with strong downward recoil soon tore the guts out of the army's boats, but Porter's schooners held up. He installed a solid platform of logs and stone for each of the heavy siege guns, and this installation proved to be more than adequate in the six days' bombardment that followed.

A few days earlier he had sent a coast survey ship to mark off exact ranges for the mortar bombardment. In spite of constant attack by Rebel sharpshooters, and the removal at night of almost all range markers established during the day, Porter's surveyors did a fair job.

The mortar boats were camouflaged with treetops and branches in their masts as they moved into position. Two divisions were anchored on the west side near Fort Jackson behind a screen of trees. The third division moored on the east bank at a range of about three thousand yards from Fort Saint Philip, but this group could not find adequate shelter and soon was bombarded by the fort's big guns. Shortly after Porter opened fire he had one ship sunk and another damaged on the eastern bank, causing him to drop back and move to safety on the left bank during the night. The mortar schooners banged away for six days and nights, giving the Confederate garrisons little time for sleep. Near the end of the bombardment, Brigadier General Duncan, commander of Fort Jackson, wrote General Lovell a graphic account of life in a fort under fire: "Heavy and continued bombardment all night and still progressing. No further casualties except two men slightly wounded. God is certainly protecting us. We are still cheerful and have an abiding faith in our ultimate success. We are making repairs as best we can. Our barbette guns are still in good working order. Most of them have been disabled at times. The health of the troops continues good. Twenty-five thousand 13-inch shells have been fired by the enemy, thousands of which fell on the fort. They must soon exhaust themselves; if not, we can stand it as long as they can."

On the night of the twentieth, Commander Henry H. Bell with gunboats *Itasca* and *Pinola* slipped upriver on a dangerous mission. His task was to break the chain barrier that stretched across the river just below Fort Jackson. Under heavy fire he succeeded in breaking only a portion of the obstruction before one of his boats went aground. Bell would have set fire to the remaining hulks, but was afraid that the illumination would give Confederate gunners a chance to destroy his grounded boat. Porter increased the tempo of mortar fire to distract the Confederates, and with this support Bell finally managed to get his stranded boat free. Farragut spent a miserable, anxious night listening to the gunfire against Bell's group, and recorded that he "never felt such anxiety in his life," waiting for

Bell's safe return. The next morning showed that the night's work had been worthwhile; the opening in the barrier was wide enough to permit Farragut's warships to pass in column formation.

However, Farragut would not start his fleet through until he was completely ready and had favorable weather. During the twenty-first, twenty-second, and twenty-third, there was a strong wind blowing downriver, bringing an unusually swift current. This was definitely not the time to make a "dash" past the forts, and the delay gave Porter an opportunity to continue his harassing fire. It also gave Farragut's ships time to make careful preparations for defense. They hung sheet cable over their sides, packed clothes bags, hammocks, sacks of sand, and ashes around their boilers and machinery spaces. Some rubbed their ship's sides with mud and marked off passageways, guns, anchors, and ammunition with whitewash to make them visible in the dark.

Farragut held frequent conferences with his captains. Finally, on April 20, he issued an operation order for running the forts. He explained that he intended to adopt a combination of two plans—his own and Commander Porter's. "The forts should be run," the order read, "and when a force is once above the forts to protect the troops, they should be landed at Quarantine, from the Gulf side, by bringing them through the bayou, and then our forces should move up the river, mutually aiding each other . . ."

He divided his force into three divisions with the following sailing order:

FIRST DIVISION—FLAG OFFICER FARRAGUT
Hartford, 24 guns; *Brooklyn,* 22 guns; *Richmond,* 24 guns.

FIRST DIVISION GUNBOATS—CAPTAIN T. BAILEY
Pensacola, 24 guns; *Mississippi,* 17 guns; *Cayuga,* 2 guns; *Oneida,* 9 guns; *Varuna,* 10 guns; *Katahdin,* 2 guns; *Kineo,* 2 guns; *Wissahickon,* 2 guns.

SECOND DIVISION GUNBOATS—CAPTAIN H. H. BELL
Iroquois, 7 guns; *Sciota,* 2 guns; *Kennebec,* 2 guns; *Pinola,* 2 guns; *Itasca,* 2 guns; *Winona,* 2 guns.

Giving Captain Bailey's gunboat division the lead through the narrow opening in the chain barrier, Farragut and his division followed, with Captain Bell bringing up the rear. Bailey was instructed to pass close by Fort Saint Philip, while Farragut concentrated on Fort Jackson. Bell was ordered to take his gunboats upriver as fast as he could during the big ship bombardment.

The plan also included Porter's force of mortars and armed steamers despite the fatigue after four consecutive days of bombardment. Porter was assigned the task of enfilading the Rebel water battery with armed steamers, while his mortar schooners increased their rate of fire on the forts to assist Farragut's passage. The armed steamers were rather well gunned and equal to the job. They were: *Harriet Lane*, 3 guns; *Westfield*, 6 guns; *Owasco*, 2 guns; *Clifton*, 7 guns; *Miami*, 5 guns; and *Jackson*, 7 guns.

At 1:55 A.M. on April 24, the flagship *Hartford* hoisted two red lanterns, Farragut's signal to get underway and execute his plan. Some ships had difficulty weighing anchor, and held up the force until about 3:00 A.M. Fifteen minutes later the little *Cayuga* slipped through the barricade opening into a hail of gunfire from Fort Jackson. She was hit forty-two times during the fifteen minutes it took to pass through the danger area, but her casualties were only six men wounded. Her commanding officer, Lieutenant N. B. Harrison, had his crew lie down on deck until the *Cayuga* was broadside to Fort Saint Philip and then suddenly they manned their guns for a furious ten minutes' fight against the fort's batteries. Safely by the forts, the *Cayuga* was the first of Farragut's force to meet the Confederate River Defense Fleet, which was standing by just above Fort Saint Philip.

The *Pensacola* and the *Mississippi* were next through the barricade, where they found an inferno of smoke, fire, and destruction. In the ensuing action several ships lost their bearings, some went aground, and the *Brooklyn* actually missed the opening in the barrier and rammed into the chained hulks. The *Pensacola* fought her way past Fort Saint Philip after a false start which took her over toward the western bank and exposed her gun crews to a cross fire from both forts. She had a narrow escape with the "pigmy monster," the Confederate ram *Manassas*, which General Lovell hoped would sink many of Farragut's wooden ships.

The ironclad ram next headed for the paddle-wheeler *Mississippi*, steering for her port paddle wheel. Commanded by young Lieutenant George Dewey, the old ship dodged successfully, and followed the *Manassas* when she slid past.

Captain H. H. Bell was an eyewitness to the events that followed, and reported to Farragut: "I witnessed the decisive manner with which Commodore Melancton Smith, in the noble old steamship *Mississippi*, met the 'pigmy monster,' the *Manassas*, the Confederate armored ram. The *Mississippi* made at her, but the *Manassas* sheered off to avoid collision and landed on the shore, where her crew escaped over the roof, the *Mississippi* pelting her meanwhile with her heavy guns."

It is interesting to note that the future hero of Manila Bay, George Dewey, was the only officer on the *Mississippi* to be singled out by Melancton Smith for praise in his report of the battle: "I have much pleasure," he reported, "in mentioning the efficient service rendered by Executive Officer George Dewey, who kept the vessel in her station during the engagement, a task exceedingly difficult from the darkness and thick smoke that enveloped us from the fire of our own vessels and the burning gunboats."

The *Hartford* opened fire on Fort Jackson at 3:55 A.M., delivering one of the most accurate broadsides of the war, justifying Farragut's reputation as a fleet gunner without peer.

Suddenly the Confederate tug *Mosher* pushed a fire raft against the flagship, forcing Captain Richard Wainright to take evasive action. In his haste he ran the *Hartford* aground within range of Fort Jackson.

The tug kept pushing its fire raft against the wooden ship. Flames began to roar up the *Hartford's* port side and reach her rigging. From his position aloft, Farragut shouted: "Don't flinch from the fire, boys. There's a hotter fire . . . for those who don't do their duty." These firm orders had a steadying effect, and soon the *Hartford's* gunners beat off the fire raft and sank the *Mosher*. Fire fighters put out the fire and the *Hartford* backed down full. The flagship trembled and shook, and just when the Chief Engineer thought that her boilers would burst, she slid off the bank and slipped past Fort Saint Philip to safety.

Next to run the gauntlet was the *Brooklyn*, commanded by Captain Thomas Tingey ("Terrible Tommy") Craven, who had run into the chained barricade and was having a difficult time. "For a few moments," he reported, "I was entangled and fell athwart the stream, our bow grazing on the left bank of the river. Whilst in this situation I received pretty severe fire from Fort Saint Philip. Immediately after extricating my ship from the rafts, her head was turned upstream, and a few minutes thereafter she was feebly butted by the celebrated ram, the *Manassas*. She came butting into our starboard gangway, first firing from her trapdoor and within about ten feet of the ship, directly toward our smokestack, her shot entering about five feet above the waterline and lodging in the sandbags which protected our steam drum. I had discovered this queer-looking gentleman while forcing my way over the barricade, lying close into the bank, and when he made his appearance the second time I was so close to him that he had not an opportunity to get up his full speed, and his efforts to damage me were completely frustrated, our chain armor proving a perfection to our sides. He soon slid off and disappeared in the darkness." The *Brooklyn* then ran past the forts with little damage and joined Farragut upriver where the Confederate River Defense Force made a last gallant stand.

These little ships, some of them "cotton clad" with bales of cotton for protection, put up a terrific fight, suffering three times as many casualties as the defending forts. Action started in the early light of dawn and ended by 8:30 A.M. with almost complete annihilation of the Confederate ships. While the river craft were hopelessly outclassed, they still fought desperately. They did manage to sink one Federal ship. The *Governor Moore* rammed the USS *Varuna* twice, and dealt her a fatal blow with a surprising innovation. At close quarters where his pivot gun could not bear on the *Varuna* under his bow, Confederate Lieutenant Beverly Kennon fired down through his own ship into the Yankee vessel. The *Varuna* hauled off in a sinking condition but kept firing until water reached her gun batteries.

When the one-sided battle ended, the *Governor Moore*, *Manassas*,

Stonewall Jackson, General Quitman, Resolute, Star, Breckinridge, Warrior, Phoenix, and the tugs *Mosher* and *Belle Algerine* were destroyed or out of action. The gunboat *Jackson* with Confederate General Lovell aboard and the passenger boat *Doubloon* escaped and made their way back to New Orleans safely. The *Louisiana, McRae,* and *Defiance* anchored under the protection of the Confederate forts.

Farragut had surprisingly few losses during the wild night—36 killed and 149 wounded. General Duncan's garrisons had 11 killed and 37 wounded. The greatest casualties were suffered by the River Defense Force, which had 74 killed and 72 wounded—a mute tribute to the gallantry of the rivermen and New Orleans volunteers who took on a hopeless engagement without flinching.

The Union fleet anchored near Quarantine to bury their dead and make emergency repairs. Leaving two gunboats to cover General Butler's landing and to assist the troops with the Confederate forts, Farragut pushed on toward New Orleans. The city was a mass of confusion. All night long levees were bright with flames and citizens burned supplies that would fall to the Yankees. Mobs roamed the streets. One thousand men volunteered to board passenger ships and fight it out in a hand-to-hand battle aboard the Union men-of-war. Fortunately for them the plan fell through, for they would have been slaughtered at long range.

As smoke settled on the levee during the morning of the twenty-fifth, Farragut's ships steamed around the bend below New Orleans. With a few well-placed shots, he silenced the small Confederate batteries at Chalmette and anchored off the city. High water in the river raised the level of Farragut's guns to a point where they dominated the city. New Orleans was helpless, and all that remained was to effect its formal surrender.

Captain Theodorus Bailey went ashore to demand surrender and the lowering of the Confederate colors, but he could not find any elected official who was willing to take the responsibility. Finally the City Council resolved that: "Having been advised by the military authorities that the city is indefensible, we declare that no resistance will be made to the forces of the United States."

A few chores remained. Porter had been left behind below the forts to assist General Butler in seizing these fortifications and occupying the city. The impatient Porter demanded that Confederate General Duncan capitulate, and when he received an unfavorable reply, resumed his mortar bambardment until he ran out of ammunition. Still the forts held out. Butler's troops took station upriver on both banks, successfully cutting off all chances of retreat toward New Orleans. At midnight on the twenty-seventh, Confederate troops in Fort Jackson mutinied against their officers and half of the garrison marched out and surrendered to Butler's troops. The next morning Porter saw a white flag waving above Fort Jackson, and General Duncan came aboard the *Harriet Lane* for surrender ceremonies. As these discussions were going on, someone set fire to the *Louisiana, Defiance,* and *McRae* to prevent their capture. An orderly rushed in to tell Porter that the *Louisiana* was on fire and drifting down on the *Harriet Lane.* "This is sharp practice," Porter told the Confederate officers, "but if you can stand the explosion we can." Shortly thereafter his flagship rocked with the blast as the *Louisiana* exploded but not an officer from either side left his chair.

General Butler assigned troops to garrison the forts and took the rest of his men up to New Orleans in riverboats which Farragut had commandeered. On May 1, he moved into the city and took over its administration. The occupation army quickly restored order and established a military government that lasted throughout the war.

The New Orleans campaign was a brilliant victory that justified Secretary Welles' fondest hopes. The North had two new heroes to cheer. The names of Farragut and Porter were on everyone's lips, and the Union navy was hailed across the country. The fall of New Orleans burst the Confederate bubble in international waters. Confederate agents trying to obtain recognition from England and France suddenly found doors closed against them. French newspapers believed that the capitulation of New Orleans meant the death of the Confederacy. The threat of diplomatic intervention disappeared, and the North was able to finish the war without any outside interference.

⚓

EIGHT

The Vicksburg Campaign

THE Union campaign to gain control of the middle Mississippi River is loosely called by historians "The Vicksburg Campaign." This series of land and naval actions lasted for a year and a half, and stretched from Cairo, Illinois, to New Orleans—a distance of about one thousand river miles. The Federal navy played an important role in the campaign, capturing several strong points such as Island No. 10, Fort Pillow, and Memphis, and assisting the army with heavy attacks at Port Hudson and at Vicksburg.

Prominent navy leaders in river actions included Farragut, Foote, Porter, and Davis, each of whom has an honored place in history. Ships used by these commanders ranged from Farragut's seagoing battleships to the "Pook turtles," which first saw action at Fort Henry. Many strange craft, weapons, and tactics emerged in this long river campaign. Charles Ellet's "tinclad" rams, unarmed swift vessels with metal-covered rams in the bow, attacked like swordfish, slashing the bottoms out of the Confederate river fleet at Memphis. Confederate torpedoes (now called mines) were used extensively, and sank the USS *Cairo* in the first successful use of the weapon in history. Farragut's struggle to move his large ships upriver from New Orleans to Vicksburg was an epic of seamanship unparalleled for frustration and triumph over overwhelming obstacles. Naval action on the river ran the gamut of the known forms of sea warfare and introduced some new ones. There were gun and mortar bombardments, surface engagements, deliberate ramming attacks, the use of a dummy warship, the introduction of mines, and even a daring rescue of a navy flotilla by an army detachment under General William Tecumseh Sherman.

After early growing pains the army and navy learned to live and fight together in the closest cooperation and mutual support. The Union's success in joint operations caused Confederate Navy Secretary Mallory to be criticized for being so "wretchedly ineffective on the water." Indications of the mutual respect the Union army and navy held for each other are evident from excerpts of the final reports of Rear Admiral Porter and General Grant. Porter wrote: "To the army do we owe immediate thanks for the capture of Vicksburg . . . The conception originated solely with General Grant." Grant was equally generous, saying, "The navy under Porter was all it could be during the entire campaign. Without its assistance the campaign could not have been successfully made with twice the number of men engaged."

In April 1862 Union forces hammered away at both ends of the Mississippi. While Farragut ported his large ships over the muddy bars at Southwest Pass to attack New Orleans, Foote captured Island No. 10—a formidable Confederate stronghold on the Mississippi sixty miles south of Cairo, Illinois. The simultaneous fall of New Orleans and Island No. 10 caused consternation and fear throughout the South, whose leaders realized that they were faced with a great pincer movement which would close at Vicksburg. The Northern thrust was predominantly an army campaign, but was well supported by Foote's river navy. The Southern threat on the lower Mississippi was almost entirely a naval operation since every man and all supplies had to be brought by sea from the east coast.

The greater challenge at Vicksburg was on land, but General Grant was right in giving the navy credit for a significant assist. Sea forces alone were not able to bring about the capitulation of this stubborn stronghold. Farragut managed to pass the Vicksburg defense in the summer of 1862, but the city did not fall until a year later. The admiral's dash by Vicksburg's batteries, located on high bluffs, demonstrated once more that well trained naval units could survive a close duel with forts; however, this very action showed how futile a naval attack would be if it were not supplemented with adequate strength ashore.

In order to cover the Vicksburg campaign in sequence from the beginning to the end, we must first look to Flag Officer Foote, whose ships in the early spring of 1862 were in Cairo repairing damage after the capture of Forts Henry and Donelson. When General John Pope captured New Madrid in March 1862, Foote brought his gunboats and mortars downriver to a safe position above Island No. 10 to give the general naval support. First he tried firing downstream with the *Carondelet,* whose engines were going full astern to offset the strong Mississippi current. He learned from this trial that his "Pook turtles" were well designed for this tactic. Accordingly, he anchored the rest of his ships above the formidable Southern batteries and began a long-range duel that lasted several weeks. This was a precarious move, because any damaged ships might drift downstream and be destroyed. Foote's long-range tactic proved inconclusive and threatened to end in a stalemate. In the exchange of fire only one of the gunboats, the *Benton,* was hit, and Flag Officer Foote could readily see that his own fire was not very effective against the enemy's cliff-mounted guns. General Pope soon became impatient with this turn of events, and asked Foote to send at least one gunboat below the forts as soon as possible.

On March 28 the navy commander called a council of all of his captains to discuss Pope's request, and learned that only one, Commander Walke of the *Carondelet,* believed that he could run the gauntlet. Foote agreed to let him go, but instructed him to make elaborate preparations and to make the dash at night. Walke lashed a coal barge filled with hay to the *Carondelet*'s side, and piled the superstructure with anchor chain, rope, sacks of coal, and other protective materials. The night of April 4 proved to be dark and stormy, broken only occasionally with jagged flashes of lightning, so Walke slipped downstream at full speed. He darted between the first batteries undiscovered, and was making a successful, covert dash past the middle batteries when the soot in his stack caught fire and silhouetted the *Carondelet* against the black night.

The Southerners poured out a brisk fire at the hapless ship, but most of the shots were aimed too high, and Walke made it safely to New Madrid. There he was given a rousing welcome by General Pope, who opened a barrel of whisky in celebration. The next night the *Pittsburg* also ran the forts, and the two ships joined to pour a devastating fire against the Confederate batteries. This was more to General Pope's liking, and he began to ferry troops across the river to the Tennessee side. This new development posed such a threat to Island No. 10 that, on May 7, its commander hastily decided to surrender, choosing his closest tormentor—Flag Officer Foote—as the person to receive his sword. Two days later this gallant naval commander, Andrew H. Foote, a veteran of three major engagements, was relieved due to the lingering ailment of his wounded foot.

His successor, Captain Charles H. Davis, did not have to wait long for his first action. The very next morning brought sharp action at Fort Pillow, a nearby Confederate stronghold downriver in Tennessee. Union river forces had been bombarding the fort for several weeks, when early in the morning of May 10, eight ships of the Confederate River Defense Fleet suddenly appeared around a bend of the river, and sped down on the anchored gunboats. In a daring action the swift Rebel boats closed in on the USS *Cincinnati,* damaging her with repeated ramming. Davis sent other gunboats to assist and the attackers retreated, but not before the rams had so damaged the *Cincinnati* and the *Mound City* that they had to be beached to keep from sinking.

Less than a month later, Davis exacted payment in kind with a similar surprise attack on the Confederate fleet at Memphis. Early on June 6, he surprised the enemy ships at their Memphis moorings and sank all but one in a one-hour running fight. The star of this engagement was the Ellet ram, which had been developed by Charles Ellet with President Lincoln's strong support. The rams were converted riverboats that relied on speed and a sharp, pointed iron ram for offense. They did not have guns, but were agile and fast enough to drive home crippling attacks on their slower opponents.

After the destruction of the Confederate fleet, the city of Memphis was powerless to resist further and surrendered immediately to Flag Officer Davis. Its capture was not so widely heralded as the fall of New Orleans, but it was a severe loss to the South. Memphis soon became a thriving Union army base, as well as the major repair facility for the Mississippi River Squadron.

With the fall of Memphis to the North, the strongest remaining defense on the Mississippi above New Orleans was the formidable city of Vicksburg—which had repelled combined land and river attacks for over a year. The navy soon learned that Vicksburg would not be an easy victory, and that it could not be taken by a naval attack alone. Troops were needed to carry and occupy the city. Vicksburg absorbed Porter's mortar bombardment like a sponge, and withstood the tremendous fire of Farragut's big guns, sending the crusty old veteran back to New Orleans to wait until forces suitable for a combined amphibious operation could be assembled.

Farragut's first thrust at Vicksburg began shortly after he had captured New Orleans. The orders which Secretary Welles had given him in January presupposed his success at New Orleans and directed him to proceed with a strong force up the Mississippi to "take all their defenses in the rear." At the same time these vague orders included a requirement to "reduce the fortifications which defend Mobile Bay." Farragut complained that everyone wanted his ships at once, but set about his task in the only practical way. First he sent Porter with his mortar schooners to Mobile Bay with orders to make preparations for a later attack that would be spearheaded by Farragut's big ships. Porter located sites for his mortar schooners and established buoys to guide the fleet into the bay. As a diversion he also occupied Pensacola, which was evacuated and put to the torch at the first appearance of the Union ships. This task completed, Porter fumed away the time impatiently, waiting for a Farragut who could not come.

While Porter sweltered off Mobile, Farragut took the remainder of his fleet upriver in the face of overwhelming difficulties. Of these, he later wrote to Secretary Welles: "The elements of destruction in this river are beyond anything I have encountered, and if the same destruction continues the whole navy will be destroyed in twelve months. More anchors have been lost and more vessels have been ruined than I have seen in a lifetime, and those vessels which do not run into others are themselves run into and crushed in a manner as to render them unseaworthy."

On May 20 Farragut completed the four-hundred-mile, nightmarish voyage, and anchored his battered ships below Vicksburg.

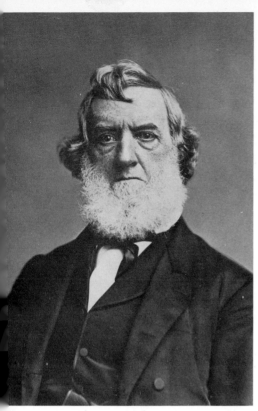

Secretary of the Navy Gideon Welles (left), and Assistant Secretary of the Navy Gustavus Fox.

Firing on the Star of the West *from the South Carolina battery on Morris Island, January 10, 1861.*

Bombardment of Fort Sumter by the batteries of the Confederate States, April 13, 1861.

The blockade-runner Lady Sterling, *which was captured by the USS* Aeolus. *This prize ship brought half a million dollars in the condemnation court.*

Captain Samuel F. DuPont (left), and Flag Officer Andrew H. Foote.

The Battle of Fort Henry. Gunboats St. Louis, Carondelet, Essex, *and* Cincinnati.

The Monitor *and* Merrimac *engagement, March 9, 1862. This painting by O. O. Davidson is from the collection of Franklin D. Roosevelt.*

Group of enlisted men aboard the USS Monitor.

CSS Merrimac.

USS Monitor.

Admiral David Glasgow Farragut. Likeness is from the last photograph from life by Chappel.

The Battle of New Orleans, April, 1862. Brooklyn, Hartford, *and* Mississippi *run past Forts Saint Philip and Jackson.*

USS Hartford, *Farragut's flagship.*

A group of enlisted men aboard the USS Hartford *in August 1864. Photo is an enlargement of a small tintype.*

Bombardment of Island No. 10 on the Mississippi by gun and mortar boats.

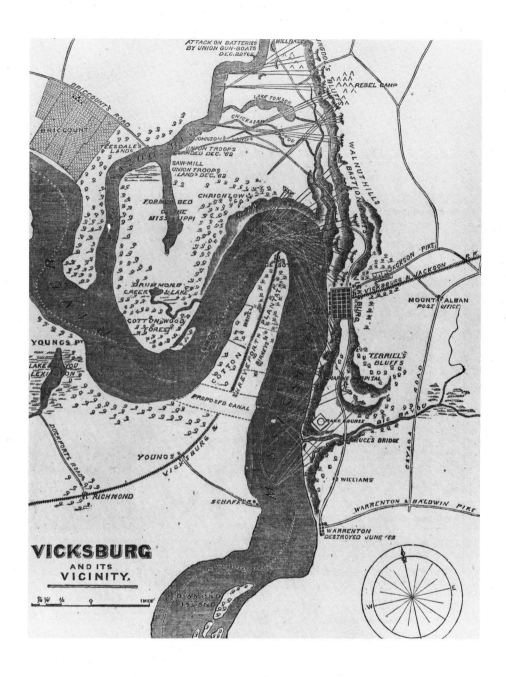

VICKSBURG
AND ITS
VICINITY.

Naval victory on the Mississippi near Fort Wright, May 10, 1862. From a Currier & Ives lithograph in collection of Franklin D. Roosevelt.

The U.S. ironclad Indianola *running past the guns on the bluffs above Vicksburg.*

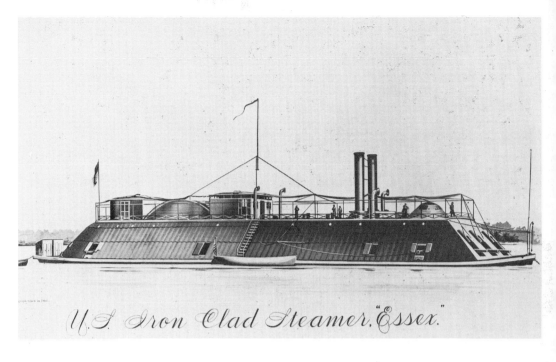

U.S. Iron Clad Steamer "Essex."

The Federal ram Queen of the West *attacking the Confederate gunboat* Vicksburg *off Vicksburg.*

CONFEDERATE GUNBOATS: "Gaines." "Tennessee." "Morgan." "Selma." MONITORS: "Manhattan." "Chickasaw." "Tecumseh." "Winnebago." Flag-ship "Hartford" and "Metacomet." "Brooklyn" and "Octorara." "Richmond" and "Port Royal." "Lackawanna" and "Seminole." "Monongahela" and "Kennebec." "Ossipee" and "Itasca." "Oneida" and "Galena." Transports. Sand Island Light.

The Battle of Mobile Bay, August 5, 1864.

THE HARTFORD AND TENNESSEE AT CLOSE QUARTERS. FARRAGUT OVERSEEING THE FIGHT IN MOBILE BAY, AUGUST 5, 1864.

Rear Admiral David D. Porter, USN

Admiral John A. Dahlgren, USN

Admiral Raphael Semmes, CSN

John H. Knowles, Signal Quartermaster, USS Hartford. *Cutlass was standard issue for bluejackets during Civil War and later.*

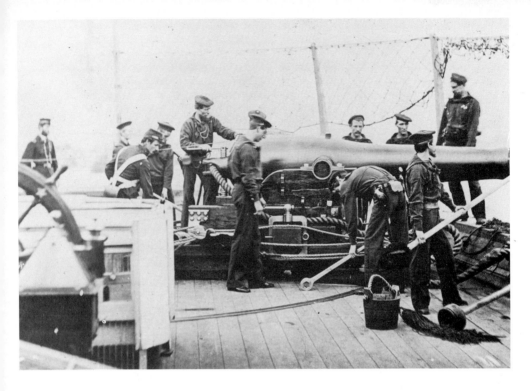

The gun crew of the USS Mendota.

Personnel of the Engineers Department aboard the USS Kearsarge, *1864.*

The USS Kearsarge.

The Confederate raider Alabama. *From a lithograph in the collection of Franklin D. Roosevelt.*

The bombardment of Fort Fisher, January 15, 1865.

Admiral Alfred Thayer Mahan, naval historian and author of The Influence of Sea Power upon History.

By this time the alarmed Confederates had strengthened their defenses by mounting eight to ten heavy guns on the two-hundred-foot bluffs near the city. Farragut's reconnaisance soon showed that he had insufficient troops to attempt a landing; his detachment of fifteen hundred men were outnumbered by a ratio of at least eight to one. Following his usual procedure, the navy commander called a conference of captains to determine his next course of action. The army troop commander, Brigadier General Alpheus S. Williams, insisted that he could not land his force until the guns on the bluffs were silenced. It was obvious to all the navy officers that their fleet broadsides could not reach the high shore batteries. Reluctantly, a sick Farragut decided not to attack. Instead he left a small force of gunboats to blockade and harass the city, and returned with his larger ships to New Orleans.

He arrived at the Crescent City on May 30, only to find emphatic instructions from Assistant Secretary of the Navy Gus Fox to return and attack Vicksburg. Fox indicated that it was the President's strongest wish that this be done as soon as possible, so Farragut had little choice but to return upriver. From his earlier reconnaissance he knew that he would need mortars for high-angle fire if he wanted to knock out the batteries on the higher bluffs. Accordingly he sent for Porter, who was only too glad to move out of miserably hot Mobile Bay for more interesting action on the Mississippi. Porter reached New Orleans on June 9, and joined the oceangoing ships in their second ascent of the mighty Mississippi. The strange armada of fighting ships, barges, and supply transports anchored below Vicksburg on June 25.

Porter went to work with characteristic energy, placing his mortar schooners in position and firing ranging shots to determine a hitting solution. At Farragut's usual council with his captains, he informed them of his plans; these were fairly simple and somewhat similar to the earlier strategy at New Orleans. He planned to get underway early enough to surprise the opposition, using heavy mortar bombardment for cover. The orders were completed and issued by the night of June 25 and Farragut's fleet got underway at 2:00 A.M. the next morning.

[91]

Porter's schooners led the way as they had done so successfully at New Orleans, opening the battle with their maximum rate of fire. Soon the terraced hills around the city began to blaze. The smoke was so thick that Union gunners had to fire at the flashes from the shore, and were unable to tell with any degree of accuracy where their shot fell. Despite their enthusiasm and their vast experience in firing great guns, fleet gunners at Vicksburg were not too successful. Shore bombardment is a difficult art under ideal conditions, even with today's guns. Captain Bell noted in his action report that the majority of the ship's fire fell on empty, unoccupied hills.

Bell's report failed to give credit to the fleet's pivot guns. Farragut's battleships and two of his gunboats were equipped with these high-angle guns which on several occasions were observed to score hits at elevations of one hundred and ninety feet. Some random shots went clear over the bluffs. The net effect of the total navy fire, pivot guns, and mortars on the bluffs, and fleet broadsides against the lower Confederate batteries, was enough to chase away the Confederate gunners momentarily, but they would return at the first lull and would take up the engagement all over again. The most troublesome defense came from a shore battery mounted high on a hairpin turn, where the river made a radical course change just above the city. In this location it could rake approaching ships for a distance of over one and a half miles. Fire from this battery caused almost all the damage sustained by the *Hartford* during the entire passage. Iron shot cut up the ship's rigging and masts and tore into the men exposed on the gun deck. Farragut's worried subordinates saved his life. They persuaded him to leave his usual perch in the mizzen shrouds just two minutes before a shot from the upper fort scored a direct hit on it.

By 6:30 A.M. Farragut's ships had run past the shore batteries and were anchored safely above the city, where they were joined by rams under command of Colonel Charles Ellet, Jr., son of the famous inventor who had been killed in the Memphis fleet action. Not all of the force got through. Actually, Farragut had not planned to take Porter's mortar schooners past the forts but he was dismayed to find

that the *Brooklyn,* commanded by Captain T. T. Craven, was missing. Porter's ships did lead the fleet in the earlier phase of the battle,
and had acquitted themselves admirably in attacks on the lower
batteries. However, Commander Porter's flagship *Octarara* lost
steering control and drifted back among the ships astern, causing
much confusion. In the midst of this melee, Captain Craven, who
had misunderstood Farragut's previous orders, became confused
himself, and instead of proceeding upriver turned back to resume
the duel with some of the shore batteries which had not been
silenced. He took two of the gunboats with him, an action which
puzzled and discouraged the tired Farragut at first, but his puzzle-
ment soon turned into rage. He sent Craven a furious letter of repri-
mand which caused the troublesome captain to resign.

The Union navy's daring dash by Vicksburg was not accomplished
without damage. The ships were struck repeatedly and suffered
forty-five casualties—fifteen killed and thirty wounded. This damage, added to that suffered at Forts Jackson and Saint Philip and,
complemented by the many collisions during the passage upriver,
made Farragut's ships a sorry sight. Battered as they were, the crews
were jubilant over their feat and were treated to an extra ration of
rum to celebrate their success.

Colonel Ellet made his smaller ships available to Farragut to run
messages upriver. The first of these was to Flag Officer Davis at
Memphis, asking him to come down with all available force to join
the oceangoing fleet. Davis arrived above Vicksburg on June 30.
The two commanders pleaded with the army for sufficient troops to
take Vicksburg. They sent a message to General Halleck who had
just occupied Corinth and was not otherwise engaged in any serious
campaign. The deliberate Halleck refused to come to their immediate assistance, but did promise to do more within a few weeks.
Although Farragut quoted the strong order of the President as his
authority for obtaining army support, none come. The landing party
commanded by Brigadier General Williams was much too small to
do any good, and over half of them were disabled by disease. Historians generally concede that a determined ground attack in force

at this time would have succeeded. If Vicksburg had been captured in the summer of 1862, it would have prevented thousands of Union casualties during the ensuing twelve months.

Davis and Farragut soon reached the obvious conclusion that since their gunboats and battleships could not scale hills or make landings against the Rebel batteries, there was nothing further they could do for the time being. Their position was becoming more and more tenuous and guerrillas and sharpshooters were plaguing them constantly from the riverbanks. Energetic troops across the hill of Vicksburg were busily installing more shore batteries, and the level of water in the Mississippi was dropping daily. This last development created a serious navigation hazard and made it imperative for Farragut to make an early decision for the disposition of his large ships.

Another peril soon appeared to challenge the large assembly of ships off Vicksburg. This came in the form of the famous Confederate ironclad *Arkansas,* which during a short life of twenty-three days caused consternation and terror in Washington official circles. Earlier in the spring, two Confederate ironclads which were building at Memphis were threatened by Davis' successful attack on Fort Pillow. In despair the Confederates had burned the *Tennessee* on the ways, but the *Arkansas* was launched and towed to Greenwood, Mississippi, for completion. Greenwood was located on the Yazoo River, which enters the Mississippi a little to the east and north of Vicksburg.

Under the capable direction of Captain Isaac Brown, the *Arkansas* moved rapidly near completion. It was a formidable ship for those waters. It had twin screws which could drive it at a speed of eight knots; it drew eleven and one half feet, and mounted ten guns in an armored casemate. Hearing of the progress that Brown was making, Farragut decided to destroy the *Arkansas* by sending the *Carondelet,* the *Queen of the West,* and two rams up the Yazoo to find the Confederate ironclad. On the morning of July 15 they met the *Arkansas* coming down the Yazoo River at full speed. The daring commander Brown had decided to make a surprise dash for the safety of Vicksburg's land batteries. In this unexpected meeting, the *Arkansas* drove the *Carondelet* ashore and chased the other ships out of the Yazoo in a running fight. Brown then moved on to surprise the rest of the Union fleet at anchor, charging into their midst with all guns firing and passing safely to the moorings at Vicksburg. Farragut was mortified at this exploit, and feared that this one ship would undo all that he had done on the river since he attacked New Orleans.

He was ready to pursue the ironclad instantly, but was persuaded to wait until nightfall while proper preparations were made. The Union force had lost more men in this one engagement than it had lost in the daring dash by Vicksburg's batteries. Brown's *Arkansas* had been struck a number of times, but his armor of railroad ties had withstood all but two shots. These penetrated the inner hull, killing and wounding several men. The city of Vicksburg celebrated Brown's feat and prepared to meet Farragut's next move. On the evening of the fifteenth, under the cover of mortar fire, Farragut got underway, using both Porter's and Davis' ships. The Union fleet delivered several broadsides into the *Arkansas* as they passed and made an unsuccessful attempt to ram. The disappointed Farragut anchored below Vicksburg and directed Porter to conduct a general area bombardment for five days, hoping that a chance shot would inflict further damage on the *Arkansas*. At least he had the satisfaction of having placed his main body between the ironclad and New Orleans.

During these trying days, Farragut received a piece of good news from the Navy Department. Congress had authorized the rank of rear admiral for the Union navy, and he was to be first promoted to that grade. Farragut accepted the promotion, but wrote that he would gladly give up his admiral's commission for the opportunity of destroying the *Arkansas*. Flag Officer Davis advised Farragut not to worry excessively over one ironclad, predicting that Captain Brown's dread ship would have a short career. This prediction proved to be true. At a time when the heroic and capable Brown was invalided and ashore with fever, other Confederate leaders decided to send the *Arkansas* downriver to relieve the siege at Baton Rouge. Despite known difficulties with her engines, the *Arkansas* brushed by the blockading ships below Vicksburg and set out for Baton Rouge, a distance of two hundred river miles. On August 5, one of the engines failed and the *Arkansas* plowed into a mud bank. The gunboat *Essex*, commanded by William ("Dirty Bill") Porter (brother of "Black Dave"), found her in this helpless condition, with only one gun able to bear in her defense. Porter attacked immediately and, in the ensuing battle, the *Arkansas* was set on fire and blown up. There was some doubt as to whether the fire was caused by the *Essex*'s batteries or whether it had been set intentionally by the *Arkansas* crew.

The destruction of the *Arkansas* and Farragut's decision to move downriver to New Orleans closed the first chapter of the Vicksburg campaign. This was a disappointing period for the fighting admiral. He had shown that his fleet could pass heavily defended land fortifications without too much difficulty, but he had been completely frustrated by the lack of army cooperation. Shortly after he arrived at New Orleans he received orders to send Porter's mortar schooners to Hampton Roads.

Farragut passed the remainder of 1862 in another period beset with difficulties with General Benjamin Butler. Butler had previously promised troops for an attack on Mobile, but had not delivered them. Also he had sent inadequate numbers of troops to Vicksburg and had failed the navy on numerous occasions. He even failed to send enough men to the naval expedition against Galveston, Texas, which could have been taken quite easily by a small force. With this lack of cooperation and support, Farragut concluded that he could best spend his time attending to the Gulf Coast blockade, which was purely a naval task.

Flag Officer Davis had withdrawn his forces upriver, first to the mouth of the Yazoo River and later to Helena, Arkansas. This separation of the fleets left an important section of the Mississippi River completely in Confederate hands, giving them access to important rail and water connections to Louisiana and Texas.

This first phase of the Vicksburg campaign, while inconclusive, marked a significant naval accomplishment. Forces under Foote, Farragut, and Davis captured and held about six hundred miles of important river communications in the heart of the Southland. From the south the navy had captured New Orleans, the principal Gulf seaport. They had proceeded upriver to Baton Rouge and patrolled the great Mississippi all the way to Vicksburg. Forces in the north had knocked out Forts Henry and Donelson, captured Island No. 10, and had taken Fort Pillow and the city of Memphis. These accomplishments on river waters deserved the highest praise and represented a naval achievement of great military and economic importance. As a matter of fact, in the entire history of naval warfare, nothing like it has been done before or since.

With the departure of the great seagoing fleet, naval support for the rest of the Vicksburg campaign fell to the gunboats of the Mississippi Squadron. The squadron was taken away from the army near the latter part of 1862. Secretary Welles was able to persuade President Lincoln and the Congress that the river force had not worked well under army administration, so it was transferred to the navy on October 1. Together with his development came one of the most amazing promotions in naval history. Secretary of the Navy Welles summoned Commander David D. Porter to Washington and told him that he was to be given the rank of acting rear admiral and that he would command the Mississippi Flotilla. For the Secretary to reach down and select a junior commander above all of the captains on the register was unprecedented, but by this time Welles had almost complete freedom in reorganizing, supplying, and directing the naval establishment. His decision was popular with Assistant Secretary Gus Fox, who felt that the river forces needed an energetic young officer who was forceful and fearless. Porter, who had been a lieutenant when the war began, jumped from lieutenant to rear admiral in two years.

He relieved Flag Officer Davis in the middle of October 1862 and immediately flooded Washington with a series of requests for more gunboats, more guns, more ammunition, more personnel—as a matter of fact, more of everything. Within two weeks, however, he reported to Secretary Welles that he was ready to support the army at any time in any operations in the Mississippi area.

The second phase of the Vicksburg campaign was a splendid example of military/naval cooperation and amphibious operations carried out with a professional flair. In early October 1862 General Grant planned another thrust at the Vicksburg area. Armies from Cairo and Memphis under Generals John A. McClernand and William T. Sherman moved south, supported in all phases of river combat and logistics by Porter's Mississippi Flotilla. General Grant planned to attack Confederate armies near Granada himself. From this city, which was about ninety miles north of Vicksburg, he hoped to join Sherman and McClernand, and move against Haynes' Bluff on the Yazoo River. If these efforts proved successful, the combined armies could then move on to attack Vicksburg from its northern flank.

In preparation for the first thrust, Porter assembled most of his squadron at the naval base in Helena, Arkansas. Then, as a preliminary move, he sent Commander Walke with a force of gunboats and tinclads to take command of the lower Yazoo River.

This led to the first recorded naval encounter against mines. The contraption was nothing more than a five-gallon whiskey jug packed solid with powder and suspended in a wooden box several feet below the surface of the water. An ingenious wire arrangement would explode a mine whenever it was tripped by a passing ship. On December 12 Walke put the *Signal* and the *Mamora* ahead of the gunboat *Cairo* and moved into the Yazoo. Suddenly a violent explosion ripped through the *Cairo*—she had tripped two of the demijohn wires. The gunboat sank in twelve minutes, without losing a single man. Stubborn Admiral Porter sent additional gunboats, including his own flagship to continue clearing the lower river. By the twenty-sixth they had completed the job, clearing the river of obstructions and dredging up mines to within twelve hundred yards of the enemy batteries at Haynes' Bluff.

General Sherman then landed a force of 32,000 men and attacked Haynes' Bluff on the twenty-ninth, but his troops were pushed back with heavy losses. While Sherman was being mauled at Haynes' Bluff, General Grant found that his own plans were going astray. His supply base had been destroyed by Confederate cavalry, so he decided to retreat rather than join General Sherman according to plan. This move spelled failure for the entire enterprise, and forced Union troops back to the Mississippi River.

To overcome the disappointment of defeat at Haynes' Bluff, Sherman and Porter immediately planned a new joint expedition against Arkansas Post, a Confederate fort on the Arkansas River. After overcoming the reluctance of General McClernand, a political general with little experience, the two professionals struck upon a mutually agreeable plan. They moved promptly in order to surprise both the Confederates and the newspapermen who traveled with their force.

With a group of three ironclads and seven light gunboats in the van, Porter led a fleet of fifty transports loaded with troops. On January 9, Sherman disembarked his troops from the transports about four miles below Arkansas Post. When everything was ready two days later, the fleet moved into close range and delivered a devastating bombardment. The heavily armored Confederate fort was holed repeatedly, and it soon became a mass of dead and wounded. In an unbelievably short time Confederate survivors waved a white flag and Porter landed to take the surrender himself. The Confederate commander, pointing to the gunboats in the river said, "How could anyone expect us to stand up against those?"

Shortly after the fort surrendered, the troops outside its walls capitulated to General Sherman. Then a race began between the army and navy to see who could get off the first battle report to Washington. The political general, McClernand, won hands down, and the first version to reach the Capital hardly mentioned the navy.

The net result of the expedition, which General Grant disapproved of and called "a wild-goose chase," was the capture of between five and six thousand Confederate troops, and the complete destruction of all supplies and ships encountered on the Arkansas River. This victory was equivalent to the capture of Island No. 10 almost a year earlier, but it did not have the same strategic value. Both Porter and Sherman made much of the expedition to overcome their failure at Haynes' Bluff a few weeks earlier. Porter was particularly proud to have sustained such light losses in overcoming an "ironclad fort," mounting a total of nineteen guns. His casualties only amounted to six persons killed and twenty-five wounded.

When the force returned to Vicksburg on January 24, Grant ordered Sherman to disembark his troops on the neck of land directly across from the city. By now he was convinced that he could not take Vicksburg from the north and that his best chance lay to the south. He fell back on the same tactics which had served so well at Island No. 10, and planned to spearhead a new attack with ships below the city's gun batteries. As a first move he tried to cut a canal across the neck of land where Farragut failed. Grant intended to use the canal for a safe troop crossing south of Vicksburg. Once this was accomplished, he saw no reason why his strong force, supported by the navy, could not carry the city. Unfortunately, the mighty Mississippi refused to be harnessed and Grant's canal was a dismal failure.

Nevertheless, Porter decided to send a part of his force down past the batteries in order to cut off the Confederate source of supplies coming from the Red River. Early in February he sent Colonel Ellet in the fast *Queen of the West* through the river defenses. The ship was hit at least twelve times with heavy shot, but the daring Ellet took time off to attack the Confederate steamer *Vicksburg* en route. Under the noses of Rebel gunners he set her on fire with turpentine balls. Once below Vicksburg, Ellet proceeded down to the Red River entrance, destroying or capturing Confederate shipping on the way. There the *Queen of the West* saw an end to her service with the Union navy. She ran aground in near a shore battery, and had to be abandoned under heavy bombardment. Confederate forces quickly salvaged the ship, and put her under the "Stars and Bars" of the Confederacy.

The *Indianola* followed the *Queen of the West* past the Vicksburg batteries on February 12, and went to her assistance. This move set off one of the most unbelievable events of the war. On learning that the *Queen of the West* had been abandoned and captured by the enemy, the commanding officer of the *Indianola* decided to return to Vicksburg. That night he was overtaken by Confederate rams and steamers filled with troops. After an hour's fight in which the *Indianola* was holed repeatedly, he surrendered when his ship was in a sinking condition. This was the only instance in the entire war

[100]

where a Union ironclad surrendered. The happy Confederates set about refloating the ironclad immediately, but on the twenty-seventh fell victim of one of the slickest ruses of the war.

In the midst of their salvage operations they were surprised by a craft that looked exactly like a monitor (ironclad). This was Admiral Porter's measure of revenge for the loss of his two ships. From an old barge he had constructed a dummy warship, using meat barrels for stacks and mud ovens with fires to make smoke. He had set the craft adrift through the Vicksburg batteries to entice the Rebels to waste ammunition. The barge survived a heavy bombardment, and drifted on downriver to the scene of the *Indianola* salvage efforts. There the *Queen of the West,* now under Confederate colors, first sighted the "monster" and dashed down to the *Indianola* to spread the alarm. The frightened salvage crew hastily set fire to the *Indianola* and blew her up. They "escaped" downriver in the *Queen of the West*. The Confederate river navy never managed to live this down.

Porter then embarked upon another somewhat scatterbrained idea, one that almost led to disaster and his own capture. He attempted to reach the upper Yazoo by cutting a Mississippi levee during high water and making his way overland through the bayous and swamps. In this venture he nearly lost a force of two ironclads and five shallow gunboats. On March 16 Porter entered the Yazoo and cut across to the north through a maze of uncharted swamp. When he had almost reached a clear stream, he was stopped by Confederate riflemen who had felled trees across his path. The Rebels then attacked with a large body of sharpshooters while Porter's ships were in a narrow channel. Cut off from ahead, and unable to find room to turn around, the gunboats attempted to back their way clear, but without success. Porter sent off a frantic message to Sherman, who was moving his troops overland a few miles away, and was rescued by an army detachment just in time. Somewhat shaken by this incident, Porter turned back and made his way slowly back down to Vicksburg without further incident.

While Porter was chasing rainbows on the Yazoo, the old professional down at New Orleans went into action again. Farragut was tired of asking the local army generals, first General Butler, and next his successor, General Nathaniel P. Banks, for troops to assist in the upper Mississippi campaign. When he heard of the loss of the *Indianola* and the *Queen of the West,* he decided that "army or no army," the time had come for the navy to move upriver once again. On March 11, he assembled four heavy ships and moved up toward Baton Rouge for a thrust at Port Hudson. His force comprised the *Monongahela,* the *Hartford,* and the *Richmond,* the old side-wheeler *Mississippi,* three 90-day gunboats, and six mortars. While it is not on the map today, Port Hudson in 1863 was an important Confederate defense. Boasting twenty-one guns and commanding a large stretch of the Mississippi just above a hairpin turn near Baton Rouge, the batteries were installed high on a bluff and were almost as formidable as those at Vicksburg.

Always one to improvise, Admiral Farragut came up with a new scheme at Port Hudson. To each of his large screw steamers, the *Hartford,* the *Richmond,* and the *Monongahela,* he lashed a gunboat on the off (unengaged) side. The gunboats were protected from enemy fire by the sides of the larger ship to which they were bound. In turn they provided emergency propulsion, were available for towing in the event of grounding, and were able to help make the sharp turn at the head of the river.

Following his usual practice, the old admiral got his ships underway for a night passage by the forts. The Confederates lit large bonfires on the banks and used metal reflectors to project the light into the river. Farragut's men were used to poor visibility, clouds of gunsmoke and confusion, but this added to their misery and to their poor performance. The ships passed close enough to the Rebel batteries to hear orders given ashore. In the melee the *Hartford* touched bottom slightly, but was assisted off the shoal by her small boat alongside and managed to make her way past the fort without any serious difficulty. The *Richmond* suffered an engine-room hit, which jammed open her safety valve and caused complete loss of steam. Her twin, the little *Genessee,* was unable to move two ships against the current, so the *Richmond* had to retreat downstream. The *Monongahela* and the *Kineo* had similar misfortunes and they too were forced to turn back.

The old paddle-wheeler *Mississippi* suffered the worst fate of all. In running past the batteries she grounded in the mud right under the nose of the heaviest Confederate guns, and was lost. The crew was forced to set the proud old ship afire and abandon her. Burning brightly, the *Mississippi* slipped off the shoal, drifted downriver, and blew up a few hours later. Of interest to U.S. Navy historians is the fact that the star performer of the *Mississippi,* who was commended for his coolness under fire, was Lieutenant George Dewey, later to win fame as the hero of Manila Bay during the Spanish-American War.

Chafing at the bit beyond Port Hudson, Farragut waited until morning to see if any more of his force would fight through. Later he moved up to the vicinity of Vicksburg to confer with General Grant and Admiral Porter. In concert they agreed that his best assist would be the blockade of the Red River, so he moved to that chore, ably assisted by two rams which Porter lent him. On April 16 Porter took seven ironclads past the Vicksburg batteries and relieved Farragut of the Red River blockade. Farragut then returned to Port Hudson to help General Banks attack that city. The first heavy attack took place on May 27, but it was beaten off by stout defense. A second try on June 14 was also turned back despite the continuous pressure of the navy ships. Matters rested at about a standstill until July 7, when word was received that Vicksburg had surrendered to General Grant; Port Hudson capitulated two days later.

Turning to the events upriver which led to final victory at Vicksburg, we find that the last combined army/navy offensive was a masterpiece of cooperation and finesse. Beginning at Grand Gulf on the twenty-ninth of April, Porter took his forces boldly into point-blank range in a hot engagement that lasted over four hours. Hampered by heavy opposition and unable to score effectively against the high gun emplacements, Porter was unable to carry the Rebel defenses. Grant met with him and decided to call off the naval attack and to move his forces across river to a more tenable position downstream at Bruinsville. Once across the river, Grant moved inland between the forces of General John Pemberton at Vicksburg and General Joseph E. Johnston at Jackson. Grant's strategy called for a feint attack at Haynes' Bluff by Sherman's troops, which he fervently hoped would prevent Pemberton from sending a large detachment to intercept him. Sherman's mock attack, supplemented by a riverboat squadron, was so convincing that General Pemberton sent reinforcements to Haynes' Bluff, leaving Grant in the position that he had sought for many long months. In a brilliant campaign he stubbornly fought his way north to Vicksburg, and then called on Porter to deliver supplies to his army near Haynes' Bluff.

As Porter's gunboats drew near Haynes' Bluff, they found that the Confederates had already evacuated most of their positions the day before. The remaining troops fled at the sight of approaching ironclads. Ironically, the formidable forts which defeated Sherman in December, now fell without a struggle. Porter then took his gunboats back to Vicksburg and supported Grant throughout the long forty-day campaign that followed. The young admiral kept up a tremendous pressure on the city with constant fire with thirteen-inch mortar shells, and landed some of his heavy guns at strategic points to supplement army artillery. At the same time his river navy kept the lines of communications open to the army's northern bases of supply.

After receiving the greatest punishment that any major Southern city suffered during the entire war, Vicksburg was reduced to rubble and its people were in a state of starvation. On July 3, convinced that General Johnston could not relieve him, Confederate General Pemberton asked General Grant for surrender terms. The proud city surrendered on July 4, 1863, and was followed shortly after by Port Hudson. The fall of these two points cleared the Mississippi from north to south, from its origin to the delta. To accentuate this momentous accomplishment, an unarmed merchant steamer, the *Imperial,* sailed from St. Louis to New Orleans unmolested during the entire eight-day passage.

As the curtain closed on the long and bitter campaign to open the Mississippi, the Union army and navy were on the best of terms and were in the closest of harmony and mutual trust. Two of the ablest army generals, Grant and Sherman, relied completely upon young Admiral Porter. This was clear evidence of his ability and justified the confidence which Secretary of the Navy Welles placed in him. Indeed, Porter had performed brilliantly; he had shown that he was an excellent leader, able to inspire loyal backing from his subordinates. He also demonstrated that he had a very good grasp of the overall strategy, a quick mind, and an ability to make decisions. Farragut felt no misgivings when he turned over the control of the entire Mississippi to Porter and took a well deserved leave of absence.

These two veterans would be star performers in later Civil War naval actions, but they move into the background during the next phase of the war which occurred at Charleston, "Cradle of the Confederacy."

NINE

Defeat at Charleston

ALARMED by the Union occupation of Port Royal in 1861, defiant Charlestonians built new defenses. They knew that in those fateful days of October, Flag Officer DuPont and General Sherman could have taken Charleston with little opposition. Fortunately for the South, these Union commanders did not realize the demoralizing effect of their amphibious thrust into South Carolina, nor did they know that almost every able-bodied Carolinian had been sent north to reinforce the Army of Northern Virginia. Instead of expanding their attack, they wasted time at Port Royal, a scant sixty miles from Charleston, and made repeated requests to Washington for reinforcements that they did not need.

The Union's indecision and apathy cost three more long years of campaigning to take the city, and gave the Charlestonians a sorely needed breather. Under the initial direction of General Robert E. Lee, and later under General P. G. T. Beauregard—a skillful tactician in his own right—the defenders erected shore batteries along the channel entrances and installed strong defenses at Forts Sumter and Moultrie. They sowed the harbor with mines and other obstructions, and in a remarkably short time the city was ready to stand off the most determined Union attack.

Confederate progress was duly noted by British blockade-runners who reported that Charleston was fast becoming impregnable. An aroused Northern public soon demanded action against this "Cradle of the Confederacy." Extremists urged the government to "Burn the hot bed of treachery . . ." and to "Plow up the ground and sow it with salt." The navy all but promised an early occupation, particularly when Assistant Secretary Gus Fox became overly impressed with the powers of the ironclad *Monitor*. He assured Congressmen that the city could be taken easily by a small force of ironclads and that soon many of these vessels would be coming off the ways. He made this promise in the summer of 1862, but it was not until the spring of 1863 that DuPont led a monitor attack against the city.

This fine seaport and symbol of the South remained one of the few harbors to serve as a haven for blockade-runners. In spite of eleven Union blockading ships, the fast Confederate steamers passed through the cordon almost at will. Southern fortifications at Sumter and along the channel shore kept the Union navy at a respectable distance outside the harbor, making it an almost impossible task to seal off the three separate channel entrances available to the blockade-runners. While the North enjoyed complete naval superiority off the coasts of Carolina, Charleston's heavy fortifications reduced this advantage and effectively stalemated DuPont and his wooden ships.

In late 1862, DuPont learned that the Confederates were constructing ironclads of their own inside the harbor, so he hastily sent word to Secretary Welles urging him to release some monitors to the Charleston Blockade Squadron. The request was made none too soon. In January the Confederate clads *Palmetto State* and *Chicora* raided the blockade fleet on station just off the Charleston entrance.

In the morning haze of January 31, Confederate Flag Officer Duncan N. Ingraham led his ship against the wooden-hulled *Mercidita,* rammed her and fired a disabling shot into her engines. *Mercidita* surrendered, and Commodore Ingraham quickly put her crew on parole and moved on to assist the *Chicora* in her engagement with the *Keystone State.* The two clads scored ten direct hits on the Union ship, killed one fourth of her crew, and disabled her engines. At one time, Commander Le Roy hauled down the *Keystone State*'s flag, but he hoisted it up again when the *Chicora* kept on firing. In spite of the reported invincibility of ironclads, other ships of the blockade force joined the fight and chased the Confederates back to Charleston. Both the *Mercidita* and the *Keystone State* were towed to Port Royal for repairs—an act considered treacherous by the Confederates in view of their previous "surrender" under fire.

This incident was seized on by commanders of both sides to gain

[107]

an advantage. General Beauregard issued an unsupported proclamation that the Union blockade had been lifted. But after careful investigation and an examination of ship's logs, Union naval authorities proved that the blockade had remained in force. In answer to Beauregard's proclamation, Flag Officer DuPont moved the monitor *New Ironsides* from Port Royal to Charleston and urged Secretary Welles to send more ironclads.

In February the monitors began to trickle into Port Royal, and DuPont decided to try them out against a Confederate fort before attempting an attack on Charleston. Fort McAllister on the Ogeechee River, near the Georgia border, appeared to be a good testing ground. It was easily accessible and was not too well defended. Accordingly, DuPont sent Commander Worden, of *Monitor–Merrimac* fame, in command of the ironclad *Montauk* and four wooden gunboats against the fort. In an exchange that lasted four hours, neither the ironclad nor the fort suffered significant damage although many hits were scored. This trial convinced DuPont that his slow-firing monitors could not defeat the defenses of Charleston by themselves and that a complete amphibious assault would be required. On the other hand, Gus Fox, who was determined that the navy go it alone without any assistance from the army, pointed out to DuPont that the monitors had survived numerous hits without casualties or damage. From their desks in Washington, Welles and Fox could not understand the reluctance of experienced naval officers to accept monitors as invincible new weapons.

On February 28 Commander Worden learned that the Confederate ship *Nashville* had grounded in the Ogeechee River near Fort McAllister. On the next day, he took the *Montauk* and three gunboats to bombard the fort and sink the enemy ship. At a close range of about one thousand yards, the ironclad *Montauk* quickly set the *Nashville* on fire. She blew up shortly thereafter, so Worden turned all guns against the fort. This second duel between fort and ironclad also was inconclusive; numerous shots were exchanged but there was little damage. Worden withdrew and retired down the Ogeechee River, setting off a mine directly under the *Montauk*'s hull. This caused considerably more damage to the ship than the two days' combined fire from Fort McAllister, and emphasized the great potential of mines. DuPont was quick to see this incident as an example of the hazards existing inside Charleston Harbor.

On March 3 another force of monitors entered Fort McAllister's "proving ground." Led by Captain Percival Drayton, who pressed home the attack to ranges of thirteen hundred yards, the monitors slugged it out with the fort for eight hours. Here again the ironclads were not significantly damaged, but at the same time they also demonstrated that the slow fire from their turret guns was inadequate to destroy the fort.

Nevertheless, the fact remained that none of the monitors was damaged in any of the pilot tests. This convinced Gus Fox that DuPont had no valid reason for deferring the long-awaited assault on Charleston. Accordingly, he persuaded Secretary Welles to direct the admiral to press an attack without delay.

After a few weeks of preparation and assembly of forces, DuPont was finally ready. On April 7, he took nine ironclads into the harbor, following a Farragut-type battle plan of forcing a passage to gain a position where his guns could command the city. However, there were two drawbacks. The defenses at Charleston were stronger than those of New Orleans, and DuPont did not have the determination and dash of Farragut.

Leading the attack was Captain John Rodgers in the *Weehawken*, an ironclad which pushed in front of it a "bootjack" raft invented by John Ericsson to clear the channel of mines and other obstructions. Following in column astern were: the *Passaic*, the *Montauk*, the *Patapsco*, the flagship *New Ironsides*, the *Catskill*, the *Nantucket*, the *Nahant*, and the *Keokuk*. DuPont chose a center position to facilitate signaling. After an agonizing first hour in which DuPont's ships made their way up the narrow, shallow channel with considerable difficulty, the guns of Forts Moultrie and Sumter opened fire.

The *New Ironsides* was so unwieldy that it had to anchor twice to avoid running aground. This unexpected development caused two small collisions and added confusion to the monitor line.

The lead monitors discovered that the inner approaches to

Charleston's harbor were protected by rows of casks and piles, heavy ropes, chains, and torpedoes. Captain Rodgers, considered one of the most able of the Union captains, patiently inspected the barricade while under fire, and concluded that it would be too difficult to blast through. He set off a small mine during this survey and assumed that there were many more hidden away in the obstruction. As a result of his examination, the ships of the van turned sharply away from DuPont's planned course, and headed back toward Fort Sumter. This threw the whole battle line into more confusion and exposed all ships to a cross fire between Forts Moultrie and Sumter. For fifty minutes the ironclads were subjected to terrific punishment. Confederate records show that more than 2,000 shots were fired from the forts, and Union logs reveal that only 139 shells were fired in return by the monitors. Confederate fire was heavy and accurate, scoring repeated hits on DuPont's ships.

Because of the increasing confusion, and his inability to get the clumsy *New Ironsides* to respond to its rudder, Admiral DuPont hoisted a signal to "disregard the movements of the commander in chief," and anchored. From this detached vantage point he could witness the fight in all its fury. At 4:30 P.M., sensing the danger of the cross fire, and fearful of maneuvering his ships in confined waters after dark, DuPont gave the signal to retire. He fully intended to renew the attack on the following morning, but after reviewing the battle with his captains that evening, he decided against another immediate assault.

As a result of collisions, and repeated hits which weakened armor plate, destroyed steering gear, and incapacitated turrets, DuPont's ships were in sad condition. The *Nahant* was hit thirty-six times, suffered seven casualties, a jammed turret, and numerous broken bolts. The *Nantucket* was hit fifty-one times and also had a jammed rudder. The *Weehawken* was hit fifty-three times, her armored deck was pierced, and her whole structure was weakened. The *Passaic* suffered thirty-five hits; the *Patapsco*, forty-seven hits; the *Montauk*, fourteen hits, and the *Catskill* received twelve hits. The Union force lost one ship. In spite of valiant efforts to save the severely damaged *Keokuk*, she sank the following morning just off Morris Island. With so many shots fired, it was remarkable that just one man was killed and only a few were wounded in the entire engagement.

DuPont's captains were impressed by the protective powers of their armor plate. Undoubtedly few wooden ships would have survived the hail of fire that bounced off the monitors, and they would have suffered numerous personnel casualties. Armor plating had surpassed the penetrating power of the cannon. The major damage incurred by the ironclads was caused by the impact of shells against the plate. The shot hit with stunning effect, rattling armor plate and shearing off holding bolts. Enough of this kind of punishment weakened the overall structure of the ships to a point where it was dangerous to expose them to more gunfire until emergency repairs could be made. Because of this, DuPont feared that his monitors were so weakened from structural damage that another bombardment would cause their heavy turrets to collapse through their decks.

Determined not to renew the attack and fight another engagement in which the navy would "go it alone," DuPont reiterated to Secretary Welles that Charleston would not fall unless the Union launched a full-scale, combined amphibious assault. He sent Commander Alexander C. Rhind, captain of the ill-fated *Keokuk*, to Washington to make a personal report of the battle. Rhind met with little sympathy and faced a hard audience. Welles wrote in his diary that he could not understand why DuPont had sent Rhind back "to howl," unless it were to "impair faith in the monitors." When Rhind made it plain that DuPont did not intend to renew the attack, Welles was furious. He went direct to President Lincoln and induced him to send the reluctant DuPont an order to hold his position inside the bar. Next he looked for a relief officer to replace DuPont—someone who would be more aggressive and more inclined to believe in the invincibility of ironclads.

DuPont was bitterly criticized by the press for his failure at Charleston, and throughout the North people had to forget their hopes for a quick victory. DuPont sent numerous explanatory reports to the Navy Department, but Welles would not permit them to be published. He feared that reports which even hinted that ironclads were not invincible would disillusion the populace and would

threaten his new construction program. He wrote to a tired DuPont
to say that Admiral Foote would relieve him, but unfortunately
Foote had not recovered from his leg wound and died within a
month of his new assignment. Welles next turned to Admiral John
A. Dahlgren, the Washington favorite who had access to the White
House and whom Lincoln frequently consulted on naval matters.
Dahlgren was considered the navy's foremost "scientist," and had
performed outstanding service for about ten years in the development of naval cannons. However, he had seldom left his desk during
that time and was not well suited for sea duty. In fact, he lost face
with his men when he promptly became seasick during his first
moments aboard ship.

Nevertheless, Admiral Dahlgren went right to work after relieving
Admiral DuPont on July 6, 1863. Four days later he supported an
army crossing to the end of Morris Island, sending the four ironclads
Catskill, Montauk, Nahant, and *Weehawken* to bombard Fort Wagner, which was near the northern end of the island. His ships were
under fire for nearly twelve hours and were hit repeatedly—the
Catskill received the greatest punishment, taking sixty hits in all.
Here again, as in previous engagements between monitors and land
forts, the ships were not significantly damaged, but in turn they
lacked sufficient punch to knock out the fort. During the next two
months Dahlgren continued to support the army, using his ironclads
as mobile artillery. During this time General Quincy A. Gillmore
lost sixteen hundred men in futile efforts to take Fort Wagner, but
he did obtain a good foothold on the island where he set up shore
guns. Dahlgren's ships went into action in support of these ground
operations a total of twenty-five times, concentrating their fire on
Fort Wagner, but taking punishment from other Confederate batteries in the harbor. Marines from the fleet were landed on Morris
Island and fought shoulder to shoulder with Gillmore's troops.

In late August, Union shore batteries on Morris Island bombarded
Fort Sumter incessantly, slowly reducing that masonry fort to a
pile of rubble. The navy joined in two more attacks, one on August 23
and the next on September 1, each time making an approach during
darkness. During these night operations the monitors fared better

than in earlier daylight attacks, scoring many hits on the growing pile of rubble that returned only a sporadic fire.

The campaign to capture Fort Wagner finally paid off. On September 7 the weary Confederate garrison quietly evacuated their defenses, fearing sapping operations which threatened to blow them off the island. As soon as Fort Wagner was out of the picture, Dahlgren renewed his efforts to take Fort Sumter, sending another force of ironclads in for close action that very night. The *Weehawken* went aground during the night action, and rather than leave her to be captured, six ships stayed with her until daylight. Salvage operations lasted until the afternoon, when the *Weehawken* finally slid off the mud bar, but not until each of the ironclads had received the most severe bombardment of the war from Fort Moultrie. The *Passaic* received ninety hits, one disabling her turrets, and the *New Ironsides* sustained crippling damage from a total of one hundred hits.

During the salvage of the *Weehawken*, Dahlgren noted that Fort Sumter apparently had only one serviceable gun and appeared ripe for capture. Accordingly he organized a landing party of five hundred, signaling his intentions to General Gillmore on Morris Island. The general was also organizing a landing group and he suggested that the forces be combined under one commander. Admiral Dahlgren stubbornly argued that the job required navy direction, so the two groups never joined up. Neither of the commanders realized that the enemy read every signal, having salvaged the Union navy code book a few months earlier from the sunken hulk of the *Keokuk*. So Dahlgren's landing party was greeted with withering musket fire as the first units reached the walls of Fort Sumter. It was a terrible defeat. Of Dahlgren's group four were killed, nineteen wounded, and one hundred and two became prisoners. Gillmore's force was delayed by the tide and never reached the fort.

Five months of constant action off Charleston had taken its toll in accumulated ship damage, so Dahlgren was forced to return to Port Royal in late September for extensive repair of his monitors. He knew that the Union army batteries on Morris Island could continue to exert pressure on Charleston's fortifications and discourage blockade-runners as well. No longer could those fast little ships slip by to the safety of Fort Sumter. That fort was almost completely destroyed, so much that the Confederates removed the last of their big guns to safer positions further up the channel toward the city. During the monitors' absence, old wooden ships continued the blockade, and General Gillmore's troops consolidated their position on Morris Island. For almost a year there was very little activity against the Confederate defenses.

The Navy Department finally stopped insisting that the navy take Charleston by storm. Obviously it could not do the job alone. Authorities in Washington now agreed with DuPont's first thesis that Charleston's capture required a complete amphibious assault. They turned to more important developments which demanded their attention, and their enthusiasm for punishing Charleston faded.

After completing repairs in Port Royal, Dahlgren returned some of his monitors to augment the Charleston blockade force and maintain pressure on the city. Cautioned by the Navy Department not to risk his entire monitor force in another frontal assault, Dahlgren nevertheless continued to plan for its eventuality. Meanwhile his ships supported General Gillmore's troops in sporadic raids against outlying posts, but the greatest activity came from determined Confederate attempts to sink blockading ships with new weapons.

Their first ingenious craft was a torpedo boat named the *David*. It was a cigar-shaped steamer of about fifty feet in length and seven feet in width, which was driven by a screw propeller. Its weapon, a sixty-five-pound copper-covered torpedo, was carried on a long pole that extended underwater from the bow, and was designed to explode on impact with a target vessel's sides. The little torpedo boat was almost submerged when fully manned, but it was able to make seven knots. During the night of October 5, 1863, the *David* attacked the Goliath of Dahlgren's fleet, the *New Ironsides*, as it lay at anchor off Fort Wagner.

Sentries aboard the *New Ironsides* spotted the strange craft when it was only three hundred yards away and fired on it. The resolute Confederate commander, Lieutenant Glasswell, held his course and rammed the great ironclad near its stern. The torpedo exploded, throwing up a huge column of water which fell back into the *David*'s cockpit, and down her stack, putting out fires. Helpless and under a hail of rifle fire from the Union ships, the *David*'s crew abandoned ship. All but two made it to safety, but the captain and a fireman were taken prisoner. Two members of the crew returned aboard and managed to get the little craft underway for a safe return to Charleston. At first the *New Ironsides* appeared little damaged and the ship's company ridiculed the Southerner's new method of attack. However, later examination showed that several bad leaks had developed, requiring a period in dry dock for repair. The little *David* joined the Confederate arsenal of mines and other effective new machines of war, but the most revolutionary of them all—the first submarine—was next to come.

Pioneer work on submarines began in New Orleans under the direction of Captain Horace L. Hunley, but Farragut's swift capture of the Crescent City forced the submariners to move to Mobile Bay. Here their strange craft demonstrated its ability to sink two barges by diving under them while towing astern a torpedo that exploded on contact with the barge. The first submarines were living tombs for all men but the captain who took position in the conning tower had a reasonable chance for escape in the event of unexpected disaster. He operated the fins which controlled vertical action, and steered the ship from his conning position. The crew furnished "Norwegian steam" by turning a hand crank connected to the vessel's screw propeller. The Confederates were elated with their first successful demonstration and Hunley was anxious to try out his ship on one of the wooden blockade fleet outside Mobile Bay. However, he received orders to take his entire force to Charleston forthwith, so he loaded the sub on a freight car and set up new operations in South Carolina in the fall of 1862.

There followed a series of tragic mishaps which would have dismayed and disheartened any but the most tenacious or foolhardy. On the maiden voyage in Charleston Harbor, Hunley's submarine was swamped by the bow wave of a passing steamer and sank to the bottom. Only the commanding officer, Lieutenant Payne, was able to swim to safety. Undaunted, the Confederates raised the little ship, reconditioned her, and obtained another volunteer crew. With Payne at the helm once again, the craft made its way as far as Fort Sumter and was again swamped. The fortunate Payne and one crew member were the only survivors. Raised and refitted once more, the craft left under command of Captain Hunley. It dived under a Confederate ship as a demonstration and never came up. All hands perished this time. Still, the Confederates were willing to give it one more try, but this time they handled their craft as if it were a torpedo boat, operating on the surface, but flooded down so that it gave very little freeboard. This time the craft, now christened the *Hunley,* carried a torpedo on a spar in the same fashion as the *David* had before it.

Under command of Lieutenant G. E. Dixon, an army volunteer from the 21st Alabama Infantry, the *Hunley* left Charleston Harbor at sundown on February 17, 1864 and headed for the harbor mouth. One of the Union navy's newest steam sloops, the *Housatonic,* lay quietly at anchor directly in the *Hunley's* path. Sentries spotted the torpedo boat when it was a scant one hundred yards away, and the *Housatonic* hastily slipped her cable, backed her engines, and tried unsuccessfully to avoid the attack. It was too late. The *Hunley* crashed into her amidships, exploding the spar topedo against the *Housatonic's* wooden hull and that ship sank in five minutes, taking the ill-fated *Hunley,* with her fifth crew, to the bottom for the last time. This startling demonstration of a new weapon encouraged later attempts to build true submersibles, but the tragic loss of life in each *Hunley* venture forestalled further action for several decades.

Nothing more of significance occurred around Charleston Harbor until the arrival of General William Tecumseh Sherman, after his triumphant "march to the sea." The Confederates managed to build two more ironclads which they never used, but their mere existence held down a considerable force of Union monitors until the end of the war, proving the validity of the concept of a "fleet in being." Naval officers conferred with Sherman in Savannah and learned that he planned to march north, bypassing Charleston en route. He turned down Dahlgren's proposal for a naval attack on Fort Moultrie, advising patience. He predicted that Charleston would fall like a ripe plum once his army had cut off all communications. Sherman was right. On February 18 the Confederates evacuated Charleston, and Dahlgren took his monitors in to occupy the city without any opposition. A week later he took over the nearby port of Georgetown on Winyah Bay.

An analysis of the long siege of Charleston must give credit to the Confederates, who succeeded in holding off a superior force of "invincible" ironclads for years. Moreover, the defense at Charleston was well directed, alert, and Rebel gunfire was most effective. On the other hand, credit is also due the Union navy for its dogged persistence in operating new and strange craft against one of the most heavily fortified cities of the age. The monitors were unbearably hot and miserable, they were vulnerable to mines and rough weather, and were veritable tombs for unlucky crews who served in them against such obstacles.

Once the army occupied Morris Island and established batteries in Fort Wagner, the value of Charleston as a port of entry disappeared. No longer could saucy blockade-runners thumb their noses at the Union fleet outside the harbor, and run to the safety of Confederate batteries. However, halting trade at Charleston meant little to Northerners who wanted to see the proud city itself humbled in defeat. To them, and to most historians, the Union navy met defeat after defeat at Charleston—the city that managed to remain a symbol of defiance until the closing days of the Civil War.

⚓

TEN

Victory at Mobile Bay

EARLY in 1862, when the Union fleet moved against New Orleans, Admiral Farragut's orders from Secretary Welles directed him to take the city of Mobile as soon as New Orleans was occupied. At the time this was excellent strategy, for the South had depleted its man-power by sending off the flower of its youth to fight in Virginia and Tennessee. Mobile's defenses were crumbling ruins, and there were no experienced military officers available to defend the city. How-ever, Lincoln became obsessed with the river war and ordered Farragut up the Mississippi to aid the army's campaign against Vicksburg. Two long years were to elapse before Farragut had an opportunity to say, "Damn the torpedoes . . ." at Mobile's entrance.

During this interval Mobile became the most important Southern port on the Gulf, serving as a port of entry for swift blockade-runners from Havana, and as an occasional haven for Confederate sea raiders. By the time Farragut had left Vicksburg and had returned with his battered ships to New Orleans, the entrance at Mobile Bay bristled with strengthened defenses. At the channel entrance there were three masonry forts, trenches, and minefields. In the bay above were three small but effective Confederate gunboats, and intelligence reports told of a huge new ironclad under construction one hundred and fifty miles up the Alabama River at Selma. Commander David D. Porter had reported in May 1862 that Mobile would fall like "a ripe plum" to a determined naval attack, but by fall it was a different story. No longer could Mobile be taken cheaply, and the Union navy was wise enough not to attempt it with an insufficient force.

The eastern side of the main channel was guarded by Fort Morgan, largest and strongest of the three fortifications. Fort Mor-gan had forty-five guns arranged behind piles of sand bags, in three masonry tiers. Outside the walls of the fort there was a strong water battery that commanded the channel entrance. West of the channel lay Fort Gaines with twenty-six guns, protected by two miles of shallow water filled with obstructions. Farther west and guarding the shallow Mississippi Sound was Fort Powell, a barely finished and lightly fortified defense on a sandy island.

In addition to these conventional defenses, the Confederates, under the wise direction of their most senior and experienced naval hero, Rear Admiral Buchanan, had planted a field of one hundred and eighty mines right under the guns of Fort Morgan. Buchanan left a three-hundred-foot sweep clear in the main channel to permit friendly traffic through, but he was certain that Morgan's guns would halt any enemy penetration through this opening. The distance was almost point-blank range, and Morgan's well trained gunners boasted that they could knock a barrel out of the water at a distance of a thousand yards.

While Mobile girded itself for an attack, Farragut had to content himself with routine blockade operations until he could assemble a proper force. His persistent requests for troops fell on deaf ears, however, and he was equally unsuccessful in his effort to obtain ironclads from the Navy Department. Feeling in ill health after the strain and difficulties of the Vicksburg attack, and foreseeing no early improvement in his situation, Farragut went on a well deserved leave of absence, taking his flagship, the *Hartford,* to New York.

During the winter of 1863, disturbing news drifted north from Selma and Mobile. The *Tennessee,* the mightiest Rebel ironclad of them all, was nearing completion. Southern naval authorities boasted that it would drive away the blockading force at Mobile, move quickly to Pensacola, recapture Fort Pickens, and then either proceed north around the Florida peninsula or return up the Mississippi to relieve New Orleans. Such talk as this was too much for an old sea dog like Farragut; he cut his leave short and departed from New York in January 1864. When the *Hartford* arrived off Mobile, Farragut learned that the *Tennessee* was not yet a serious threat because it was unable to cross the sandbar that separated the upper and lower sections of Mobile Bay. He learned also that other ironclads were building at Mobile, so he renewed his request for monitors.

The small Confederate navy in Mobile Bay was highly trained and efficient. The converted river steamers *Morgan, Gaines,* and *Selma* had black-painted sides greased with tallow and looked for all appearances like ironclads. But it was the monster *Tennessee* that represented the greatest challenge to Farragut's wooden ships. This new ironclad, a smaller and more maneuverable replica of the *Merrimac,* measured 209 feet in length and was 48 feet wide. Armed with two 7-inch and four 6-inch Brooke rifles and protected with six inches of iron armor plate backed by wood, she was almost impregnable. However, the optimistic Farragut noted that the *Tennessee* could only make six knots, was sluggish in comparison to his own ships, and that she had the usual weakness of Confederate ironclads —her rudder chains were partially exposed and vulnerable. Weeks went by as Farragut assembled his ships and made preparations for the attack. He studied various courses of action carefully. He was perhaps the most experienced man of the age in combating land defenses, having successfully run by Forts Saint Philip and Jackson at New Orleans without losing a ship. Twice he had passed by the strong batteries at Vicksburg, and he had taken his flagship *Hartford* by the defenses of Port Hudson. While in all of these actions he had attacked at night, the minefield at Mobile Bay eliminated this tactic. Farragut decided that he would have to move through the main channel in daylight in order to have the best chance of avoiding the minefield. Recalling how he had lashed two ships together at Port Hudson for mutual protection and additional propulsion, he decided to use that tactic again at Mobile Bay.

Calling his captains together in conference to outline his plans, he informed them that he would get underway at 5:30 A.M. on D day, and would run past the forts and destroy the Rebel ships in the bay beyond. This was a classic Farragut tactic—bold, daring, and precise. Nothing was left to chance. His ships were thoroughly stripped of extra gear; anchor chains were lashed over the side near the engines, and piles of sandbags and coal were placed around gun openings. Each large ship was mated with a weaker gunboat on the off side away from Fort Morgan's guns, the two being lashed securely so they could maneuver as one. Asked by one captain if he could give his crew a tot of rum at reveille, Farragut replied that he could not. Instead he told his captains to issue every man two cups of good coffee at 2:00 A.M., and that at eight o'clock he would pipe all hands to breakfast in Mobile Bay.

Farragut's battle line consisted of two columns. In the van were his four monitors, *Tecumseh, Manhattan, Winnebago,* and *Chickasaw,* a little ahead and to starboard of the squadron of wooden ships. The latter column had seven pairs of ships lashed together: *Brooklyn* and *Octorara, Hartford* and *Metacomet, Richmond* and *Port Royal, Lackawanna* and *Seminole, Monongahela* and *Kennebec, Ossipee* and *Itasca,* and *Oneida* and *Galena.* For the first time Farragut did not lead the battle line with the *Hartford.* His captains had prevailed and begged him to take second position, arguing that this safer station was more suitable for a valuable commander. Farragut rued the day that he had consented to this change, for the cautious *Brooklyn* captain in the lead nearly caused disaster in a critical moment when he backed his ship to keep from entering the Confederate minefield.

At 5:30 A.M. on August 5, the flood tide was running full and there was a westerly wind to carry the smoke of battle into Fort Morgan. Farragut's fleet got underway and headed for the channel entrance. The stouthearted and stubborn veteran took his favorite fighting position in the shrouds of the *Hartford's* mainmast, completely exposed to enemy fire, and ordered a quartermaster to lash him securely so that he would not fall if stunned or if he suffered one of his infrequent attacks of vertigo. In order to avoid the minefields, each ship had to pass close to Fort Morgan and then turn to port to follow the channel. In anticipation of this maneuver, Confederate Admiral Buchanan stationed the *Tennessee* on the eastern side of the channel just by Fort Morgan, and put his gunboats on the western side where they could rake the Union ships.

A description of only the naval action at Mobile Bay would leave out one of the more important phases of the battle. Not only was this an important naval engagement, it was also a significant joint action in which Union army troops played a major role in subduing the forts.

Major General R. S. Granger arrived off Mobile on August 1 with twenty-four hundred troops, and set a fine example of cooperation in the joint venture. He agreed with Farragut that his troops should be landed at Dauphin Island to invest Fort Gaines in conjunction with the fleet attack. Assisted by gunboats, Granger landed on the island August 3, took up preliminary positions, and waited for the fleet to get underway.

On the ramparts of Fort Morgan, watching the approach of the Union fleet on August 5, stood a former U.S. naval officer and shipmate of Farragut's—Brigadier General Richard L. Page. No stranger to naval warfare and well aware of the devastating power of naval broadsides in the hands of experienced gunners, he held his fire as the little monitors steamed by, disdaining to reply to their slow-firing turrets, and waited for Farragut's battle line. Perhaps he had also done his homework, and had studied battle reports from Charleston. Time after time monitors had demonstrated their effectiveness in deflecting enemy fire, suffering as many as one hundred hits without major damage or injury to personnel. Why should he, reasoned Page, waste good ammunition against ironsides when large, fat wooden targets were only minutes away?

The monitors opened fire on Fort Morgan at 6:40 A.M., and at about seven o'clock the Confederate batteries blasted a reply at the lead wooden ship *Brooklyn*. Five minutes later the *Hartford* was in range and soon the familiar din and smoke of battle engulfed Farragut's column. Everything was proceeding smoothly and according to plan, when two sudden developments threatened the entire operation.

Captain Tunis A. M. Craven (brother of Thomas T. Craven), in the leading monitor *Tecumseh*, spotted the Confederate ironclad *Tennessee* in the bay ahead, and in his eagerness to close with the dreaded ship, altered his course away from the channel center. The *Tecumseh* cut across the corner of Admiral Buchanan's minefield, passing to the left of the red marker buoy that warned of danger!

She struck a mine and sank in two minutes, carrying ninety-three men to their death. Twenty-one managed to scramble clear.

From this incident comes one example of U.S. Navy tradition that has found a place in official annals along with such battle cries as Jones' "Don't give up the ship," and Decatur's "I have not yet begun to fight." Everyone who sailed in a monitor knew that while it afforded a miracle of protection against enemy fire, it was also an iron grave if it started to sink. The monitor's hatches were small and only a few men could pass through in an emergency. As the pilot-house of the *Tecumseh* flooded, both Captain Craven and pilot John Collins waded over to the escape hatch. "After you, pilot," said the courteous Craven, stepping aside to let Collins out. A moment later the *Tecumseh* turned turtle and took Captain Craven to the bottom.

In the *Brooklyn* Captain Alden thought that he too was headed toward mines, so he backed his engines. His smaller consort, the *Octorara*, did not hear the order and kept going ahead. This set up a twisting motion for the pair of ships and threw the *Brooklyn*'s bow to starboard across the narrow channel entrance. The channel was thus blocked by the lead ship, and the ships astern crowded forward. During this development the guns of Fort Morgan increased their fire. Disaster was imminent.

In this moment of truth with confusion reigning supreme, Farragut's mettle and leadership came to the fore. When he learned that the *Brooklyn* had backed to avoid torpedoes (mines), he shouted, "Damn the torpedoes, go ahead." The *Hartford* and the *Metacomet* turned sharply to port, avoiding the *Brooklyn* but passing directly over the minefield. Miraculously they made their way safely through and were followed by all the other ships of the battle line. When he passed over the water where the *Tecumseh* had gone down, Farragut instructed the *Metacomet* to lower a boat to pick up survivors. Seeing this act of mercy, Confederate General Page ordered his gunners not to fire on the lifeboat.

As the battle line fought its way past the forts, each ship was taken under fire by Fort Morgan and the three gunboats of Admiral Buchanan's fleet. The *Tennessee* first tried to ram the *Hartford*, who managed to evade her through superior speed and maneuverability, so the Confederate ram turned to other ships of the column as they came within range. Unsuccessful in ramming the *Brooklyn,* the *Tennessee* engaged the remaining ships with gunfire as they steamed through the channel. All of the ships were hit, but only the *Oneida* was seriously damaged. Shot from the fort struck her boiler, but she managed to keep up enough steam to pass by successfully.

When the *Hartford* was clear of Fort Morgan, she was able to drive off the Confederate gunboats with her own big guns. Farragut detached the *Hartford's* mate, the *Metacomet,* to pursue the smaller boats into shallow water. As the remaining larger ships followed through the slot, they cut loose their "mates," and soon the Union gunboats had the situation under control. The *Selma* was captured and the *Gaines* was so badly damaged that she was beached near Fort Morgan. The lucky *Morgan* also took shelter by the fort and managed to escape up the bay during the night.

The run by the forts completed, Farragut ordered his ships to anchor at 8:30 A.M. in order to fulfill his promise of a good breakfast for his men. At this point the *Tennessee* lumbered up the bay ready to take on the whole battle fleet. It is difficult to assess Admiral Buchanan's reasoning for this decision. He had more promising courses of action available. For example, having a shallower draft than Farragut's sloops, he could have entered shallow water and engaged the larger ships at long range with impunity. Or he could have remained under the protection of Fort Morgan's guns and waited for Farragut to come and get him. The *Tennessee* had to be eliminated as a threat before the Union army and navy could safely storm the forts and before they could claim to have established complete control of the bay entrance. Another more promising venture would have been to go outside the channel and engage the transports that were lying at anchor unprotected. This would have caused Farragut to run by Fort Morgan again in order to protect his flock. Instead, the brave but shortsighted Confederate commander chose to close his major enemy in one last glorious struggle. It was a fateful and hopeless decision.

Quick to see his opportunity, Farragut ordered his anchored ships to get underway immediately and to close the Rebel vessel. He recalled his monitors for the battle and signaled his larger ships to ram the ironclad. This was an optimistic order, for their wooden hulls crumpled like paper when they struck the *Tennessee's* iron sides. Moreover, their broadsides bounced off her protective iron plates with little effect. The fight soon became a confused, swirling mass of ships and smoke. The skipper of the *Lackawanna* made the mistake of ramming his own commander's flagship and was banished from the fight by an irate Farragut who ordered him to anchor out of range where he could do no more harm. It is reported that he turned to a U.S. Army signal officer who had been stationed aboard the *Hartford* to assist in signaling to the troops ashore and said, "Can you say, 'For God's sake' by signal?" When told that it could be done, Farragut then said, "Then tell the *Lackawanna*, for God's sake, to get out of the way and anchor."

Called by Farragut, "one of the fiercest naval battles on record," the action between the *Tennessee* and the Union fleet continued hot and heavy until about ten o'clock. The most punishing damage was inflicted by the monitor *Chickasaw*, whose commander, George Hamilton Perkins, stuck to a position about fifty yards astern of the *Tennessee* and fired repeatedly into her after casement wall with eleven-inch shot. This and the combined fire of the Union fleet soon began to inflict telling damage on the Confederate. Her exposed rudder chains were shot away, leaving her helpless to steer. The *Chickasaw's* guns wounded Admiral Buchanan severely when he entered the *Tennessee's* after casemate to examine the damage suffered there. With his leader out of action, and unable to turn his ship so that his own guns could bear on the enemy, Confederate Captain Johnston surrendered. His ship was leaking, her stack was riddled so that her speed was limited, three of his guns were out of action, and the *Tennessee* was filled with gas, smoke, and wounded men. Buchanan sent his sword to Farragut as a token of surrender.

The Union navy's magnificent victory was bought at considerable cost. Including the 93 men lost on the *Tecumseh*, Union losses totaled 145 killed and 170 wounded. Though Confederate naval forces were no longer a threat, the three forts still stood as a challenge to any ship that might wish to enter the bay. Farragut lost no time in attending to them. His gunboats had already bombarded Fort Powell, but he sent a monitor to speed up the operation. When the *Chickasaw* arrived to enfilade from the rear, the Confederates abandoned Fort Powell, and blew it up with time charges. Next on the program was Fort Gaines. After a full day's bombardment on August 6, the commander at Gaines surrendered, much to the disgust of General Page who was so aroused that he crossed over in a small boat to stop the proceedings. He arrived too late, however, and beat a hasty retreat back to Fort Morgan.

Page was made of sterner stuff than his subordinate commanders at Forts Powell and Gaines. When he was ordered to surrender, he replied that he would fight as long as he had the ability to resist. Farragut set his ships in position for harassing fire on August 9, and maintained a persistent and steady nuisance bombardment while Union General Gordon Granger transferred his troops from Dauphin Island to the mainland. Here they took up position against Fort Morgan and added their mortar and artillery fire to the bombardment. This combined attack began on August 21. In another day of unceasing bombardment by both fleet and army units, Fort Morgan slowly lost its punch. Its walls were breached in several places and soon only two guns were left in condition to fire. Confederate General Page decided that he could not resist further, and surrendered after an honorable defense on August 23.

News of Farragut's victory reached Washington through the devious route of the Confederate newspapers. General Butler noted it in the Richmond *Sentinel* and telegraphed word to Washington, where it cheered a despondent city, weary with war. Shortly thereafter General Sherman took Atlanta, and President Lincoln ordered a one-hundred-gun salute fired at the Washington Navy Yard in celebration of the two joint victories.

The triumph of Mobile Bay did not mean immediate capture of the city. There was no need to sack Mobile, because it had lost its importance. No longer could blockade-runners ply their illegal trade at Mobile's docks, nor could the dreaded sea raiders enter for rest and refit. Mobile was merely another town that waited for capture, unimportant to the Confederate cause. All eyes of the North and

South now moved to the one remaining Southern port still open for trade—Wilmington, North Carolina.

Mobile Bay brought an end to the active career of Admiral David Farragut, who was relieved shortly thereafter to proceed to Washington. One of the Union navy's greatest leaders, Farragut was at his peak at Mobile. Here he showed all the genius and attributes of a skillful tactician, as well as his ability to make correct decisions at the height of battle. He was cautious and careful in preparation, but bold in attack, exposing himself courageously in some of the sharpest naval gunfire in history. His determination to win and his resolute, stubborn courage in pitting his antiquated wooden ships against dangerous land fortifications and ironclads set a splendid example for generations of naval officers to follow.

⚓

ELEVEN

Wilmington Captured

DURING the latter part of the war, Lee's Army of Northern Virginia depended almost entirely upon the port of Wilmington, North Carolina, for supplies. Shoes, rifles, leather, ammunition, blankets, meat, coffee, and saltpeter poured into Wilmington, while cotton and turpentine were shipped out in payment—the Union blockade notwithstanding.

It remained the last busy, vital Southern port until General Grant made available sufficient troops for an assault on its defenses in late 1864. Operations against the city's approaches required the largest fleet ever assembled during the Civil War, and its investment saw one of the most poorly coordinated Union amphibious ventures, and also one of the best. The first attack on Christmas Day resulted in ignominious withdrawal, but the second attempt three weeks later was a masterful demonstration of victory through joint land-sea operations.

Wilmington's geographical location resembled that of Mobile. With strong defenses at the mouth of the Cape Fear River, and additional batteries and obstructions along the inner approaches, the city itself rested securely about twenty-eight miles upriver. Two forts guarded the sea entrance: Fort Caswell to the southwest; Fort Fisher to the northeast. These formidable defenses kept Union blockading ships from pursuing the small, fast blockade-runners upriver, and provided a safe anchorage where runners would wait for dark or foul weather before darting past the blockade.

Public opinion in the North slowly blazed to fury as boatload after boatload of contraband supplies were unloaded at Wilmington's groaning piers. Several Congressmen demanded Secretary Welles' resignation. The Northern press accused Union naval officers of plotting with the blockade-runners for financial gain. Each successful penetration of the blockade was taken by the navy as a personal affront. The blockade commander, Rear Admiral Samuel P. Lee, reported that the only way to alleviate his situation would be to destroy Forts Fisher and Caswell so that his ships could effectively put a cork in the bottleneck approaches of the Cape Fear River.

Secretary Welles repeatedly asked the War Department for sufficient troops to capture the forts. Although President Lincoln agreed with Welles on the importance of the project, he refused to interfere with the army's plans; it was not until Gus Fox made a personal visit to General Grant in September 1864 that the navy received assurance of army support. Fox returned from the front lines to Washington with Grant's promise that twelve thousand troops would be available in October. Grant had made two stipulations to his promise. First, he demanded that Admiral Lee be relieved of duty in favor of a more energetic and daring naval officer; and second, he stated that the plans for the attack had to be made in utmost secrecy. Both of these requirements were to haunt the naval secretaries.

Admiral Lee (grandson of Richard Henry Lee) had close family ties with important men in Washington, and he was quite senior on the navy's officer rolls. To find his relief without hurting his feelings was a touchy problem that required careful planning. Gus Fox hit upon the ideal solution—he would have Lee and Farragut swap jobs. Farragut had just won the Battle of Mobile Bay and had very little to do. Lee was an able administrator, if not a fighter, and was competent to carry out routine operations for naval forces in the Gulf. However Farragut, in ill health and worn out by a succession of strenuous campaigns, begged off.

Welles looked over his officer lists again and reluctantly decided upon Rear Admiral "Black Dave" Porter. General Grant gave his enthusiastic approval, having had extremely good luck with Porter in the Vicksburg campaign. Porter, who had risen from a senior lieutenant at the beginning of the war to flag rank in two years, was resented by senior officers in the navy. Yet he was the type of man who could demand and get fanatic loyalty from younger officers, and he was a successful combat leader who had come through in many varied and trying situations. The confident Porter studied Wilmington's defense and reported to the Secretary that he could bottle up Wilmington if given sufficient naval forces and thirteen thousand troops. He got the job and took command of the North Atlantic Blockading Squadron in October 1864.

Porter's dash and energy pumped new life into the fleet, which had been following a desultory blockading routine for a long time. An outburst of Confederate activity in the Roanoke River in the Albemarle Sound area gave his men an opportunity to demonstrate their newly found spirit and reckless disregard for danger.

With the aid of an ironclad built on the Roanoke River, the Confederates had soundly whipped a group of gunboats and had driven Union forces from the town of Plymouth, North Carolina. After this activity, their ironclad the *Albemarle* was berthed behind a barrier of logs near the city, and it remained a serious threat to any further Federal activity in the area. This constant thorn in the Union navy's side inspired one of Porter's more adventurous officers to develop a scheme for her destruction. Lieutenant William B. Cushing proposed to copy the Confederate tactics which had been successful in Charleston, by attacking the *Albemarle* with a *David*-type spar-torpedo boat.

Porter gave his consent, and on a dark night in October, Cushing took a fast steam torpedo boat up the Roanoke River. He was discovered as he drew near his target, and was greeted with a hail of rifle fire as he bored in on the ironclad. Charging at full speed, Cushing skipped over the logs and found himself right under the *Albemarle*'s side. He coolly lowered his spar and exploded the torpedo under the Confederate's bottom. Their ironclad began to sink, but her crew on the deck continued to fire into the torpedo boat. Cushing took the only possible course of action, and ordered his men to abandon ship and swim for the two Union gunboats that had accompanied him upriver. He and one seaman escaped, but two of his crewmen were killed and the remainder were captured. In recognition of his daring feat, Cushing received the thanks of Congress, was spot-promoted, and became the captain of Admiral Porter's flagship.

By late October the Union fleet was ready to sail against Wilmington, but General Grant refused to send the promised troops. Somehow news of the expedition had leaked to the newspapers, and it became breakfast-table conversation both above and below the Mason-Dixon Line. Grant waited until December before he released the army detachment to Generals Weitzel and Butler, who were to direct the land operations at Fort Fisher.

Porter's task was not an easy one. Fort Fisher was the strongest single fortification that the Confederates had erected in the entire war. Located on a narrow tongue of land, it had a face almost one mile long on the shoreline, and a shorter face across the end of the peninsula. This massive pile of palmetto logs and sand was a scientific series of bombproof shelters, trenches, minefields, and guns. Its main battery of forty-four heavy guns were mounted in barbettes; and there were numerous smaller guns strategically located. Despite its size, Fort Fisher required only a relatively small number of troops; it was garrisoned with nineteen hundred in December 1864. It was obvious to Porter and his army commanders that Fort Fisher could only be taken by an infantry attack and that could not be launched until its heavy walls were breached by fleet bombardment.

While more experienced sailors and soldiers were making plans for a "conventional" attack, General "Ben" Butler hit upon the idea of taking the fort with a "secret weapon" and carried everyone along with his enthusiasm and powers of persuasion. He proposed to load a ship with explosives and blow it up adjacent to the fort, expecting the force of the blast to either flatten the walls or to stun the garrison into submission. Porter went along with the idea, primarily to humor the army and to avoid difficulties in obtaining adequate numbers of troops for his expedition. He gave Butler the *Louisiana*, an old hulk of a ship which displaced about two hundred and fifty tons. It was loaded with one hundred and fifty tons of powder and equipped with complicated detonating devices. In this new era of development which featured the ironclad, the mine, and the submarine, anything that was novel and showed some promise of success received fairly enthusiastic backing.

The ensuing preparations for Porter's first assault resulted in a miserably planned affair which was earmarked for defeat before it started. In the first place, there was no love lost between General Butler and Admiral Porter, who had had their differences two years earlier at New Orleans. While the fleet units and army transports assembled off Fort Monroe in Hampton Roads, there was ample opportunity for the leaders to confer and draw up joint plans, but the expedition got underway in early December with only the skimpiest of understandings. They agreed upon Beaufort, North Carolina, as the staging area into Wilmington, but Porter's fleet took one route from Norfolk to Beaufort, and Butler's transports took another. In the bad weather that occurred during their separation, the two major units lost contact and searched in vain for one another off Beaufort. By the time they made a rendezvous, they had lost several days of good weather and Butler's transports had to enter port for fuel and supplies. They were pinned down there by a series of storms until the impatient Porter took his fleet south to the entrance at Wilmington, leaving word for Butler to follow.

During the night of December 23, Commander Rhind and thirteen volunters took the powder boat *Louisiana* to a position about three hundred yards off Fort Fisher. This was an act of consummate bravery—one that compares with Lieutenant Hobson's attempt to block the Spanish fleet at Santiago, Cuba, thirty-five years later. The crew of the *Louisiana* faced the danger of a premature explosion from enemy fire, a collision with its towboat, or accidental detonation from some of the devices on board. Luckily they got the old craft with its dangerous cargo into her slot without any mishap or opposition. Not trusting the mechanical clock detonators to do the job, Commander Rhind built a fire and set off slow powder trains before leaving. Shortly after 1:00 A.M. on the day before Christmas, the *Louisiana* exploded in a firecracker display; it burned with a spectacular blaze, but did not produce the expected shattering blast. Sailors aboard distant fleet units scarcely felt the shock, and no one in Fort Fisher was disturbed. In short, the "secret weapon" was a fizzle.

Porter then set about the capture of Fort Fisher by more conventional means, taking his fleet in at close quarters for the most ambitious mass shore bombardment in naval history. He anchored a division of ironclads on an arc near the fort and placed divisions of gunboats and frigates on wider arcs beyond. Each ship was given a segment of the huge wall for an assigned target. The bombardment commenced at noon on December 24 and lasted until sunset, when Porter ordered his ships to withdraw for the night, convinced in his own mind that he had all but destroyed the fort and that it would fall easily before a determined army attack. However, Butler arrived late in the afternoon and was not ready to land until the following day. His reconnaissance showed considerably less damage to Fisher's walls than the navy claimed, so he persuaded Porter to resume fire for the Christmas Day assault. Under the protection of another massive bombardment by fleet units, Butler managed to land about two thousand troops through the heavy surf, but a combination of events influenced him to withdraw without launching an attack. In the first place, he was disappointed with the effect of Porter's bombardment and noted in his report that only two of Fisher's guns had been destroyed. Then there was a gathering storm, which threatened to force a general exodus of the fleet. This would leave his troops ashore in an untenable position, completely vulnerable to counterattack.

Porter was furious at Butler's decision, and soundly criticized the reluctant general in a series of dispatches to Washington. Later investigation into the matter proved Butler to be right in one respect. According to Colonel Lamb, the Fort Fisher commander, Porter's first bombardment had caused a few spectacular fires but had not done serious damage to the main fortification or the guns. Had the expedition begun with better planning and exchange of ideas, Union forces could have landed in good weather during early December and the outcome might have been different. As it turned out, the Christmas Day assault was a bitter disappointment which was difficult to explain to the higher authorities.

Butler departed in his transports, but the stubborn admiral refused to give up. He kept his fleet in ready position at Beaufort and appealed to Washington for more troops. His old friend General

Grant came to the rescue, writing to Porter to "hold on, . . . I will send you more troops, with a different general." Grant chose Major General Alfred H. Terry, an officer of proven ability in combat, and directed him to cooperate with Porter, adding that he could trust the admiral implicitly.

Terry took over the detachment of sixty-five hundred troops that had suffered through the first attack on Fisher, and Grant gave him fifteen hundred more experienced combat men. With this group loaded into transports, General Terry arrived at Beaufort to join Porter on January 8, 1865. In an aura of newborn confidence and cooperation, the two leaders and their staffs sat down and planned the next assault. Porter's orders for bombardment were reproduced in number and distributed throughout Terry's key commands. Complete details of the army landing and attack were given to Porter's division leaders. When the conference ended the two leaders had produced the most complete and comprehensive plan for joint action of the Civil War.

Once again the attack was delayed by storms, but the weather cleared sufficiently to permit a joint sail from Beaufort on January 12. Navy gunboats delivered a preliminary bombardment to clear the beaches near Fisher on the morning of the thirteenth and landing operations commenced at 9:00 A.M. In one of the finest landings in military history, General Terry put eight thousand men ashore, completely supported with ammunition, mules, food, and essential supplies in six hours. By 3:00 P.M he set his men to digging trenches against an attack from the mainland and stationed the remainder of his force in preliminary positions near the great walls of the fort. A determined Confederate attack at the beginning of the landing might have turned the tide, but there were too few Rebel forces available. Moreover, the guns of Porter's huge fleet discouraged any such attempt. Throughout the day, navy guns poured out a thunderous bombardment against the great fort. This time Porter changed his bombardment plan from one of area fire to one of specific target assignments. Each ship was given several targets with orders to keep firing until their targets had been destroyed.

The navy attack continued on the fourteenth while General Terry consolidated his position and waited for the bombardment to knock out the big confederate guns. Porter sent the ironclads *New Ironsides, Saugus, Canonicus, Monadnock,* and *Mahopac* to anchor at positions averaging eight hundred yards from Fort Fisher, much closer than that of the first attack in December. The rest of his armada followed in behind, taking up position on arcs that covered the entire fort face. Under this terrible bombardment at close range the defenses of Fort Fisher began to crumble. Confederates who watched the onslaught from across the Cape Fear River wondered how any of their men inside the fort could survive this "storm of gunfire."

By previous agreement the general assault was to commence on the fifteenth, with army troops charging the long face of the fort and a landing party of marines and bluejackets storming the short face across the tip of the peninsula. Porter's landing party consisted of sixteen hundred sailors and four hundred marines. Unfortunately the sailors were armed only with pistols and cutlasses, a throwback to the old days of boarding parties at sea, but hardly suitable for an attack of this kind. The sailors looked upon the whole affair as a lark, laughing and joking until they were cut down by a murderous fire from the fort parapets. The party landed about two miles from the fort walls and waited until 3:00 P.M. for a coordinated attack with General Terry's troops. Colonel Lamb and his Confederate defenders mistook the landing party as the main assault, and crowded into the short face of the fort to concentrate on this hapless group. In a display of excellent gunfire and control of fleet bombardment, Porter continued to pound away at Fisher until the last minute. At the signal of ship whistles and sirens, both the army and navy detachments launched simultaneous attacks.

Captain Dawson, in charge of the marine detachment, had orders to cover the main assault by the sailors. Commander Kidder R. Breese hastily assembled his bluejacket force, which was composed of landing parties from thirty-five different ships—men who had been at sea for months and who had never drilled together. It was one of the bravest and most futile landing efforts in naval history. At the sound of the whistle, the sailors cheered, waved their ships' banners, fired their pistols vainly in the direction of the fort, and raced down the beach with drawn cutlasses. The leaders halted just in front of Fort Fisher's corner, where the two wall faces joined, and waited for stragglers to catch up. Here they fell under a concentrated hail of rifle fire from the high wall, but they rallied and followed Ensign Robley D. Evans toward a breach in the wall. Trapped by ditches and other obstructions, the leaders were shot down to a man.

The landing party had 350 casualties—80 killed and 270 wounded, before it fell back to a position of safety on the beach. In the final moments the entire group panicked and fled unashamedly away from the bloody massacre. Their effort was not in vain, however, because it created a diversion which permitted General Terry's army troops to reach Fort Fisher's walls unmolested. Actually, the first soldiers to pour through a breach fired into the backs of Confederates who were fighting off the navy landing party. The tide of battle turned and swept back into the fort's interior. With savage fury Lamb's men stalled the Union attack and General Terry called on Porter for gunfire support. Just how Porter's gunners managed to achieve such pinpoint accuracy with their old guns bobbing around on the lazy North Carolina swells is hard to explain, but target practice and experience paid off. Fleet gunfire staggered the Rebels and gave Terry a chance to bring more troops through Fisher's breached walls. By late afternoon half of the fort was in Federal hands, but it was not until 9:00 P.M. that the last Confederate group was rooted out of Fisher's bombproof shelters. When the fighting ceased General Terry counted over 2,000 Confederate prisoners, and sorrowed over 540 casualties in his own force.

After the fall of Fort Fisher, Wilmington was doomed. Across the river Rebel units blew up Fort Caswell and retreated toward the interior. Porter sounded out the main channel, set up buoys, and sent his gunboats upriver under Cushing to investigate. He was amazed at the depth of Wilmington's defenses, but felt no haste in pushing on to final victory. Practically, his fleet now controlled the river entrance and this halted blockade-running for good.

In a month-long campaign which saw continued cooperation between army and navy forces, Wilmington finally surrendered to Admiral Porter. Gloom prevailed over the South and General Lee's fate was sealed. Cut off from his last remaining source of foreign supply, and unable to obtain any from a Southland devastated by Sherman's march to the sea, he lasted only three more months and surrendered to General Grant at Appomattox in April 1865.

The end of Wilmington marked the final major action of the Union navy and also the finish of Admiral Porter's role as a combat leader. In spite of all his faults, history marks Admiral David D. Porter as one of the country's great naval heroes, equal in his attainments to his father before him. Admittedly he was boastful, and he was prone to gloss over details. His battle reports always showed himself in a favored light. He stepped on senior officers' toes and was often rude to army officers whom he thought to be incompetent. Yet his record speaks for itself. He was one of the most successful combat leaders of the war, and he ran a taut outfit, whether it was a small group of mortar schooners, a division of riverboats, or the largest fleet ever assembled. He was a tough, fearless officer when the chips were down, and he maintained a clear head in the midst of roaring conflict. Never did he falter in his love of country or his devotion to his service. Younger officers were inspired to great deeds by his example and leadership, while his detractors, both those in blue and gray, often cursed him. Secretary Welles had misgivings whenever he assigned Porter an important job, and undoubtedly would have selected a more "compatible" type if one had been available, but he knew that Porter would pursue any assignment to a successful conclusion. These constant successes were more important than his personal shortcomings.

A description of the navy's role in the Civil War is incomplete if it is limited to coast and river action. Throughout the battles and campaigns described in previous chapters ran a thread of conflict on the high seas. Some of the most interesting events of the war occurred far from the shores of the United States.

⚓

War on the High Seas

THE Confederate navy's primary task was the defense of thirty-five hundred miles of Southern coastline. It was absolutely essential for Southern ports to remain open so that "King Cotton" could be used in exchange for war supplies from abroad. To defend the coast, Confederate Secretary of the Navy Stephen R. Mallory pursued three courses of action simultaneously. First, he cooperated with the army in river and harbor defense. Second, he persuaded Jefferson Davis to authorize privateering by the navy and the Southern merchant marine. And last, he loosed raiders on the high seas to seek out and destroy Yankee ships wherever they could be found.

By all rights each of his missions was doomed to failure, but in reality each came within a hair's breadth of succeeding. Naval minefields almost kept the Union navy away from Southern ports, sinking twenty-seven ships and frightening the Union sailor half out of his wits. If these amateurish mines had been a bit more sophisticated and reliable, they might easily have sunk Farragut's entire fleet at Mobile Bay. Ironclads built for the specific purpose of raising the blockade nearly swept Union ships before them. By the luckiest coincidence, the little *Monitor* arrived in Hampton Roads just hours before the *Merrimac* steamed majestically out for her second "field day" with the Union's wooden ships. If Lieutenant Catesby Jones had not been opposed that day by Worden in the *Monitor*, he would have repeated the triumph of the previous day and driven every wooden blockading ship away from Norfolk. Ironclads at Vicksburg, Charleston, and Mobile performed valiant service for the South and likewise came within an ace of victory.

Confederate privateering was authorized in April 1861. Private parties (anyone who owned a boat that could mount a gun) and small ships of the Confederate and various state navies all joined in the early effort. Even some unscrupulous Yankee whaling captains made inquiries and offered to join the Southern cause in search of rich booty and prize money. At the outset it appeared that privateering would accomplish its purpose and that frightened Northern merchants would force the Union navy to drop the blockade in order to protect sea lanes. However, the Federal blockade slowly closed off ports of entry, and by 1863 had a stranglehold across the broad reaches of Southern coasts. Privateering quickly disappeared and never again was a viable threat.

Confederate cruiser raiders caused staggering losses to Union commerce on the high seas. They all but chased the flag of the United States from the oceans, and caused marine insurance rates to skyrocket. The feats of these raiders were amazing and have never been equaled in the history of naval warfare. Actually, there were only five raiders that were reasonably active, and no more than two of these conducted their raids during the same time interval. Yet among them these sea wolves captured or destroyed 260 merchant vessels valuing about $20,000,000. When the Civil War began, the United States was second only to England in the size of her merchant marine, and the American flag waved proudly in ports and sea lanes all over the world. The Confederate cruisers destroyed about five per cent of the Union merchant fleet and drove another half in panic to neutral registry. This was a blow from which the American Merchant Marine has never recovered to this day.

The South's able Navy Secretary, the prime mover of these pigmy efforts against the giant Union navy, was an ideal choice for his post. Stephen Mallory was born in the Florida Keys and was reared in a world of tall ships, hurricanes, shipwrecks, and salvage. He was elected to the United States Senate in 1851, and soon became well known in Washington circles for his ability and knowledge of the sea. He was appointed chairman of the Senate Naval Affairs Committee, and was serving in that post when Florida seceded from the Union. When he resigned from the Senate and moved back to Florida, Jefferson Davis persuaded him to accept an appointment as Secretary of the Navy for the Confederacy. Energetic, experienced and confident, Mallory knew his job. He was full of ideas and completely conversant with all new developments in naval operations and construction. Convinced that President Lincoln's blockade, the "Anaconda Plan," would slowly squeeze the life out of the South, he bent most of his energy towards its destruction. Since his efforts in coastal defense have already been described, the majority of this chapter will be devoted to Confederate privateering and the saga of the *Alabama*—the greatest raider of them all.

REBEL PIRATES

The legal points of Confederate privateering have been argued for years, but in the final analysis it is generally conceded in the court of world opinion that the South did not break international rules. Privateering was a traditional American practice, which was used effectively against England in 1776 and again in 1812. Actually, it is one of the few recourses that a nation, feeble at sea, can use against a stronger opponent. In past history of the United States, privateering had been a profitable enterprise which had attracted numerous capable seamen in search of quick riches. In the War of 1812, over five hundred ships had operated under American letters of marque and prowled the oceans in search of British shipping. England's losses in that war ran into millions of pounds, and the protests of English merchants helped create an atmosphere conducive to the Treaty of Ghent in 1814. President Jefferson Davis hoped to repeat that performance in 1861, but the practice of privateering was gradually drifting into international disrepute, and adventurous seamen found that blockade-running was a less hazardous and more lucrative occupation.

Popular opinion in the North influenced a wave of indignant protest after Rebel privateers made their first catches. President Lincoln was moved to issue a proclamation branding individuals who participated in such acts as pirates, and Gideon Welles made numerous references in his war diary to the nefarious rogues and scoundrels who sailed in these miserable little ships. In the relative quiet some twenty years after the Civil War, however, James Russell Solely, a scholarly naval historian who served as Assistant Secretary of the Navy rendered the following opinion:

THE ESSENCE OF THE PRIVATEER LIES IN ITS PRIVATE OWNERSHIP; ITS OFFICERS ARE PERSONS IN PRIVATE EMPLOYMENT; AND THE AUTHORITY UNDER WHICH IT ACTS IS A LETTER OF MARQUE. TO CALL CRUISERS PIRATES IS MERELY TO MAKE USE OF INVECTIVE. MOST OF THEM ANSWERED TO ALL LEGAL REQUIREMENTS OF SHIPS OF WAR; THEY WERE OWNED BY THE GOVERNMENT, AND THEY WERE COMMANDED BY NAVAL OFFICERS ACTING UNDER A GENUINE COMMISSION . . . NEITHER THE PRIVATEERS, LIKE THE "PETREL" AND THE "SAVANNAH," NOR THE COMMISSIONED CRUISERS, LIKE THE "ALABAMA" AND THE "FLORIDA," WERE GUILTY OF ANY PRACTICES . . . CONTRARY TO THE LAWS OF WAR.

While privateering had been outlawed by the Treaty of Paris in 1856, the United States had not been a signer to that declaration. This moved Captain Raphael Semmes to suggest to a member of the Confederate Congress that the South adopt a system of privately armed ships. Calling it an irregular force similar to the militia system on land, Semmes went on to say:

PRIVATE CUPIDITY WILL ALWAYS FURNISH THE MEANS FOR THIS DESCRIPTION OF WARFARE, AND ALL THAT WILL BE REQUIRED OF YOU WILL BE TO PUT IT UNDER SUFFICIENT LEGAL RESTRAINTS TO PREVENT IT FROM DEGENERATING INTO PIRACY, AND BECOMING AN ABUSE. YOU COULD HAVE A LARGE IRREGULAR SEA FORCE TO ACT IN AID OF THE REGULAR NAVAL FORCE, SO LONG AS THE WAR LASTED, AND WHICH COULD BE DISBANDED, WITHOUT FURTHER CARE OR EXPENSE, AT THE END OF THE WAR.

Acting under poor advice, President Lincoln made a halfhearted attempt to scotch Southern privateering by threatening to hang any persons captured in the pursuit of this practice. He argued that the Confederacy was not a *de facto* nation and, therefore, had no right to issue letters of marque. He actually approved court proceedings to try some of the first prisoners from privateers for piracy, but had to back down when Jefferson Davis quietly mentioned retaliation.

Davis ordered captured Union prisoners in Richmond to draw lots to see who would be hung in retaliation, on a one-for-one basis with the prisoners being tried in New York. The whole matter suddenly was hushed, and the prisoners in question were exchanged.

Under Davis' proclamation, about thirty craft of all description, generally river steamers of light draft, mounting one or two small guns each, were issued letters of marque. As these ships were let loose to prowl off the Mississippi Delta, the Virginia Capes, Boston, and even the approaches to New York, mayors of seaport cities, insurance representatives, shipowners, and merchants made loud protests to Washington against Gideon Welles' naval strategy. They pointed out that he had made no provision for protecting valuable property from depradations of "pirates" on the high seas. The Secretary refused to change his plans and withstood a torrent of abuse that would have ruined and disheartened a lesser man. He was criticized, lampooned as the Rip Van Winkle of the cabinet, and threatened bodily harm, but he refused to budge from his conviction that the blockade was the most important single task of the Union navy.

The Confederate privateering venture might have been more successful if there had been more ships available for that purpose. Not only was there a finite number of suitable ships, but also there was only a small seafaring population to man them. Nevertheless, the first efforts of the privateers were quite successful. Later on it became exceedingly difficult for the "pirates" to bring their prizes back into Southern ports because of the blockade. Secretary Mallory and President Davis were unsuccessful in their attempts to obtain international recognition and to establish prize courts in distant shores. In spite of difficulties some ships made rich hauls. The brig *Jefferson Davis* made a seven-week cruise from Cape Cod to Trinidad, and captured ten merchantmen. The *Calhoun* captured the Yankee ship *Ocean Eagle* off the Mississippi entrance on May 16, and by the twenty-ninth had taken five more prizes. The *Savannah* took a prize off the coast of Charleston, but was herself captured shortly thereafter. The privateer *Petrel* was also captured by the USS *St. Lawrence*, and the privateer *Beauregard* was picked up a few months later by the USS *Anderson*. The privateer *Dixie* made a four-week cruise out of Charleston and returned safely with three prizes. As mentioned earlier, there were three very successful privateers that operated out of Hatteras Inlet with impunity until the Union navy, under Flag Officer Stringham, closed off the entrance in August 1861. These were the *Winslow,* the *Raleigh,* and the *Beaufort*—all sailing under the North Carolina navy until July, when they were transferred to the Confederate navy.

The Confederate hopes that these depredations would break the blockade through indirect pressure never materialized, but Gideon Welles did relent enough to send out as many as eight ships to track down the brig *Jefferson Davis.* While there were only a handful of privateers in the business, they managed to capture between fifty and sixty merchantmen. It is evident that a larger and more intensified effort by Confederate privateers would have had a profound effect eventually on the Northern blockade. However, as the raiders themselves suffered attrition through shipwreck and capture, there were no other ships to take their places. Privateering died a quick death, but not before it had given Northern merchantmen and coastal cities a few bad months.

THE *TRENT* AFFAIR

In the confusing months of 1861, with Welles' first feeble blockading effort and Mallory's persistent but puny attempts to thwart it, there occurred an incident on the high seas which almost changed the course of the war. In April Secretary Welles had called home almost every ship from foreign station, but he left some units in the West Africa Squadron on patrol against slave trade. Those ships that did return were cautioned to keep a sharp lookout for Confederate privateers and cruiser commerce raiders. One of these was USS *San Jacinto,* commanded by Captain Charles Wilkes, which put into Cuba for coal during the last part of her return voyage. Wilkes had been alerted to the operations of Raphael Semmes in the *Sumter,* and was keeping a weather eye peeled for this first Confederate cruiser to venture into blue waters. He failed to find the *Sumter,* but his keen nose for trouble unearthed another adventure which the fame-loving commander thought to be equally attractive.

At Cienfuegos he learned that two distinguished Southerners were bound for England as special Confederate emissaries. They expected to depart from Charleston for an intermediate point and then to take passage in an English ship to Liverpool. James M. Mason and John Slidell were ex-U.S. Senators and men of prestige, wealth, and influence who could accomplish many things in European countries which were already sympathetic to the South. Mason had been appointed minister plenipotentiary to Great Britain, and Slidell was designated special emissary to France. The North was outraged at the prospect of having these two men in the courts of Europe, and Lincoln's administration made feverish efforts to prevent their passage. Wilkes immediately forgot all about the *Sumter* and concentrated on intercepting the two agents who were almost in his backyard.

Mason and Slidell had indeed begun their journey. At Charleston they waited for about three weeks for an opportunity to escape through the blockade on the Confederate cruiser *Nashville*, but none came. Secretary Welles had ordered more ships to Charleston to tighten the blockade there, and had actually sent one sloop to the English Channel where it could lie in wait for the *Nashville* should it break by the blockade. In view of all these precautions, the two agents chose instead to charter the famous blockade-runner *Theodora* to take them to Cuba. They arrived in Havana in mid-October with their families and secretarial staffs, and were greeted as ambassadors of a powerful country. In the round of parties which followed, neither made any secret of plans to continue their journey on the British mail packet *Trent*. The *Trent* would take them to St. Thomas where they could board a larger steamer to England.

While Mason and Slidell were being entertained in Cuba, Captain Wilkes pondered his situation, weighing the pros and cons of international law that would apply should he stop the *Trent* and seize the two agents. Before the radio was invented, communications at best were poor. Commanding officers of ships on distant station had to rely on their own judgment to a greater extent than now. The major source of news was the newspaper, or an exchange of gossip with another ship which they might happen to meet at sea. Little time was available to request instructions from higher authority, so the commanders had to act on their own judgment and trust that their decision was correct. Wilkes decided that the agents could not have valid passports since the Confederate States of America was not a recognized country in the international community. Accordingly, he planned to halt the *Trent* during her passage through Old Bahama Channel. He was on firm ground in exercising his right to stop and search a nonbelligerent ship on the seas in time of war, but he was dead wrong in forcibly removing personnel from that ship. The United States had already fought two wars to uphold the principle of freedom of the seas, and it was foolhardy of Wilkes to disregard past history.

Nevertheless, the *San Jacinto* intercepted the *Trent* on November 8, firing a shot across her bow to bring her to heel, and exploding a second shell a scant hundred yards from her beam when the *Trent* ignored the first warning. Wilkes sent a boarding party with instructions to ascertain if Mason and Slidell were on board. If they were, he instructed his boarding officer, Lieutenant Donald McNeill Fairfax, to inform the master of the *Trent* that these men were considered contraband of war, and that the *Trent* was subject to capture. Young Fairfax had a difficult time aboard the *Trent,* suffering such abuse that he had to call in a detachment of marines to quiet things down. He was so impressed with the protests of the indignant passengers that he returned to advise Captain Wilkes against taking the *Trent* as a prize. Wilkes balked, but finally acceded to this advice; however, Mason, Slidell, and their two male secretaries were to be removed, and their families offered accommodations on board the *San Jacinto.* The Confederate agents insisted that they be removed forcibly, and told their families to continue on to England, confident that they would rendezvous with them later.

Wilkes took his prisoners to Hampton Roads and became the hero of the hour. The Northern populace, in the depths of gloom over disastrous events of 1861, brightened at this good news, and took Wilkes into their hearts. Newspapers urged the government to "Consecrate another Fourth of July to him, load him down with

services of plate and swords of the cunningest and costliest art."
Official Washington applauded at first, but then began to have misgivings. President Lincoln felt that Mason and Slidell would prove
to be "elephants on our hands, that we could not easily dispose of,"
and told Secretary Welles to move the prisoners to Boston. Welles
was extremely disappointed that Wilkes had not seized the *Trent*
so that the matter could be adjudicated in an admiralty court; but
he was delighted to find a person who demonstrated decision and
purpose, and who carried off his action successfully. He sent Wilkes
a congratulatory letter for the great public service he had performed.

It took two weeks for the news of this exploit to reach England,
and another two weeks passed before the British reaction was
known in the United States. Fortunately this elapse of time permitted some hot tempers to cool, but at first it appeared that war
with England was imminent. Secretary of State Seward was adroit
enough to realize that a dreadful mistake had been made; he quietly
set about disavowing the act while the public wildly acclaimed
their new hero. When Seward learned of the "typhoon of fury" that
swept through England after news of the affair arrived, he began to
worry. But further British acts were more menacing. Several thousand troops were sent to Canada, and an embargo was placed on
military stores being exported from Great Britain. Foreign Secretary
Palmerston's vigorously worded protest left no doubt that England
expected the United States to release the Confederate agents
promptly.

Seward handled the situation with such tact and secrecy that
neither the British nor the Yankees knew until long afterward that
Mason, Slidell, and their two secretaries were quietly released on
January 1, 1862. The agents were put aboard a British warship for
passage to England, and the matter subsided. The *Trent* affair was
the only action on the high seas which seriously inflamed tempers
and almost resulted in war with England. As the war progressed
there were other disagreements, but proper diplomatic niceties
settled these without bad feeling.

THE CRUISE OF THE *ALABAMA*

Of all Confederate efforts to wage a successful war on the sea, the commerce raiding cruisers came closest to success. Led by the *Sumter* which captured eighteen prizes in a short life span of seven months, five active Confederate cruisers exacted a terrible toll in Yankee shipping. Most famous of all raider commanders was Raphael Semmes, the "Gray Ghost" of the Confederacy, who darted across oceans unhurt and undiscovered for three years in his two commands, the *Sumter* and the *Alabama.* He overhauled and stopped more than three hundred ships of different registry, and burned almost seven million dollars' worth of Union shipping. While the *Florida* and the *Shenandoah* were successful in their own right, no cruiser captured the fancy and the imagination of the world as did Semmes' second command, the *Alabama.* The daring, astute, and pious captain of the *Alabama* hung up a record in commerce destroying that had never been equaled. He was so highly regarded by the German navy that, in later years, all officers of surface ships in the Imperial Navy were encouraged to keep a copy of Semmes' *Memories of Service Afloat* in their cabins for reference and study.

The story of the *Alabama* is the most glamorous, and its telling can suffice for the activities of all the other Rebel raiders, whose activities were similar, but not as spectacular. Curiously enough, the *Alabama*'s history begins with the end of one of her sister raiders. When Raphael Semmes was unable to obtain coal or effect repairs on the *Sumter* at Gibraltar, he was trapped by three Union warships. Rather than face certain suicide in an unequal engagement, he surveyed his rust-ridden ship and sold it to British ship owners. Semmes then proceeded to England to confer with Confederate agent Commander James D. Bulloch, and later made his way to Nassau, intending to return to the Confederacy by taking passage on a likely blockade-runner. While in Nassau he received orders from Secretary Mallory to return to England in order to take command of the *Alabama,* which was being fitted out in secrecy by the able Commander

[147]

Bulloch. At this point the *Alabama* was known as hull *290* in the yards of Laird Shipbuilders.

To all intents and purposes, the *290* was to be a merchant ship. But Bulloch and the Laird builders had contrived to construct the ship so that she had all the necessary fittings to convert her into a warship with minimum effort. They knew that it would be impossible to fit her out and commission her as a ship of the Confederate navy under the nose of Charles Francis Adams, the American Minister to England, who kept a watchful eye on all British shipbuilding. To avoid possible seizure as the *290* neared completion, Bulloch arranged for her merchant captain to sail over the horizon into the lost wastes of the Atlantic during her trial run. Under the inoffensive name *Enrica,* the future *Alabama* made for the Azores and a rendezvous with destiny. There Captain Semmes came aboard and took the ship out beyond territorial limits for installation of guns and commissioning under the Confederate flag.

In this manner the most feared of Confederate cruisers came into being. It was "Confederate" because of its registry and its Southern officers, but the crew was composed almost entirely of adventurous English and Irish toughs from the docks of Liverpool. Throughout its history, the *Alabama* was plagued with desertions among the rank and file, and even a stern disciplinarian like Semmes often had his hands full during the rigors of the ship's twenty-two-month cruise. He replenished his crew from the more daring tars aboard prizes he captured, offering good food, fair play, and a chance of prize money.

When the *Alabama*'s conversion was completed she was one of the finest ships afloat. In the words of her commander, she had the "lightness and grace of a swan." With full sail power, she was also a screw steamer that measured 235 feet overall, with a beam of 32 feet. Under a full load of coal, which would last her for eighteen days, the *Alabama* drew 15 feet. She could sail at a good ten knots, and when she "cheated" by using engines with sail, she was good for up to thirteen knots, a speed that compared favorably with that of the fastest ships of the time. For armament the *Alabama* carried six 32-pounders, three on a side, and two pivot guns. The forward pivot was a 7-inch rifled gun, while the after gun was an old smooth-bore 8-inch cannon. There were accommodations for twenty-four officers and one hundred and twenty men, machine shops which permitted Semmes to make emergency repairs far out at sea, and even an early design evaporator, capable of distilling fresh water from the sea. The ship handled easily and rode out storms without significant damage.

On August 24, 1862, Semmes commissioned his ship and hoisted the Confederate flag, but was in the unenviable position of having a ship without a crew. The original crew sailing the *290* to the Azores were guaranteed return fare to Liverpool. In a fiery and in-spiring speech, Semmes told the assembled men they were free to leave if they wished, but he offered them an attractive alternative. Double pay in gold in advance, fine rations, grog twice a day, a life of adventure aboard a ship whose mission would prevent it from engaging an enemy man-of-war if possible, and prize money. With these tactics Semmes signed on eighty out of the original crew of ninety, and set sail for the whaling grounds southeast of the Azores. For two months he worked the North Atlantic and captured twenty prizes. From his experience in the *Sumter* he knew that it would be useless to attempt to collect prize money, so he burned most of his prizes, saving one every now and then to use as a cartel ship for the growing list of passengers.

Having a ship which sailed as well as the *Alabama,* Semmes was able to remain at sea for long periods of time. This helped in main-taining discipline, and also permitted evading frequent port calls which inevitably disclosed his location. As the *Alabama*'s list of prizes grew, more and more Union men-of-war were let loose on Semmes' trail. This pleased the Confederate commander, who knew that his secondary mission was to lure as many navy ships as possible away from blockade duty. Within four weeks after the *Alabama* began raiding operations, Secretary Welles had detached a total of fifteen ships from all other duties with instructions to track Semmes down.

From the whaling grounds near the Azores, Semmes moved off the Grand Banks and conducted a flaming raid southward off the

Eastern Seaboard of the United States. His quick successes caused consternation in Washington. The Navy Department was flooded with letters and telegrams, demands, and petitions for protection of the Union merchant marine. Instead of whaling vessels, Semmes now busied himself with grain ships, burning some just off the entrances to New York Harbor. Shortly afterward he was forced to leave these lucrative waters for coal. Silently the *Alabama* headed for Martinique, the rendezvous previously given to the master of her support ship, the *Agrippina*. On learning that the USS *San Jacinto* was near the area, Semmes sent his support ship out to sea headed for a little-known Venezuelan port. When the Union sloop arrived, Semmes calmly slipped past the larger ship in the dead of night—the second time he had done so during his career as a sea raider.

Having quelled an abortive attempt at mutiny at Martinique, Semmes looked industriously for a ship carrying enough gold to pay his crew. While he felt that his stern disciplinary measures (he half-drowned some insurrectionary ringleaders) would keep them quiet for a time, he knew that a little excitement and some gold coins in their purses would ease their tempers. He cruised the Caribbean looking in vain for one of the steamers on the Panama-New York run with California gold as cargo. At last, on December 7, his lookouts sighted a large, brig-rigged paddle-wheel steamer. The excited crew of the *Alabama* closed in on their quarry with visions of huge gold ingots dancing before them.

After a stern chase of a few miles, in which the steamer would have outrun the *Alabama*, Semmes fired a shot through her rigging and brought her to heel. To his chagrin he found that he had intercepted a gold ship, but that it was on the wrong leg of the voyage. She was the *Ariel*, bound from New York to Colón with a bevy of passengers, mostly women, and a battalion of marines. Together with the crew, the ship carried almost seven hundred souls, far more than the *Alabama* could accommodate. The boarding officer returned to *Alabama* and reported that the five hundred women and children were so frightened that they bordered on hysteria. In his *Memoirs*, Semmes admitted that "the tear of a woman has always unmanned me," so he devised a scheme to calm their fears. He sent for his handsomest lieutenant, told him to put on his best uniform and sword, and sent him to the *Ariel* to coax the ladies out of their hysterics.

Resplendent in his gray and gold uniform, the lieutenant entered the ladies' cabin and assured them that they had fallen into the hands of Southern gentlemen, and that Northern newspapers to the contrary, Captain Semmes did not make war on women. Picking out the youngest and prettiest of the lot, he entered into conversation with her and soon became a favorite. The ladies crowded around him, eagerly asking questions. His air of reassurance, his good manners and charm, soon quelled their dismay and the ladies forgot their hysteria. Presently a young lady who was bolder than the rest asked the young officer if she might have one of the gold buttons from his uniform as a souvenir. Someone found a pair of scissors, and away went the button. Another and another asked for a souvenir. Semmes said, "When I got my handsome lieutenant back, he was like a plucked peacock—he had scarcely a button on his coat."

As much as Semmes wanted to burn the *Ariel,* he could not bring himself to it because of the problem of passengers. After detaining the ship several days while he searched for another vessel to capture and make into a cartel ship for the passengers, he finally released the *Ariel* on a ransom bond.

The *Alabama* rounded Yucatán on the twentieth of December, and slipped unseen into the Gulf of Mexico, bound on a mission of utmost secrecy. Semmes had read of an amphibious expedition off Galveston, and was determined to swoop down on the troop transports in a surprise attack. When the *Alabama* arrived there were only five ships in the area, and they were not troop transports but warships. Undaunted, Semmes determined to "have some sport," by decoying one of the Union warships away from the others. With careful tactics he lured the USS *Hatteras* about twenty miles from her compatriots, and turned on her suddenly during the night. In thirteen minutes, the *Hatteras* was sinking from six heavy broadsides, so her commanding officer, Captain Homer C. Blake, surrendered. Semmes launched his boats, picked up survivors, and sped away in the darkness before the other Federal ships could overtake him.

Semmes' next port of call was Kingston, Jamaica, where he landed his paroled prisoners and enjoyed a few days' rest. News of the *Alabama-Hatteras* engagement reached Washington while the *Alabama* was in Kingston. Secretary Welles was at a loss to explain how the Confederate ghost had slipped in and out of the Gulf of Mexico, which had only two entrances. Nor could he reconcile himself to the questionable activities of Admiral Wilkes, whose seven-ship squadron seemed more interested in chasing blockade-runners for prize money than in looking for the *Alabama*. One thing was certain in Washington at the time, the *Hatteras* had to be avenged.

To avoid capture by Welles' avengers, Semmes departed reluctantly from Jamaica after an enjoyable five days, and resumed his trail of capture and fire about the Caribbean. Working the trade routes vigorously, Semmes noted fewer and fewer ships of American registry. He concluded that he was working himself out of business in these waters, and headed south for the remote island of Fernando de Noronha off the coast of Brazil. This was where he had arranged another rendezvous with his faithful *Agrippina*. As luck would have it, he captured a collier en route, and took it with him as an anchor to leeward in the event *Agrippina* failed to show. In this desolate outpost Semmes had no difficulty in persuading the governor to close an eye to the rules of international law. When his support ship did not appear, Semmes quickly looted his prize, took it out just beyond the three-mile limit, and set it on fire as a spectacle for the islanders who had been so kind.

From Fernando de Noronha the *Alabama* cruised off the coast of Brazil with fabulous luck, touching at Bahía to discharge passengers and to be royally entertained. He then worked his way slowly across the South Atlantic, leaving a trail of burnt ships in his wake. On July 29, two years after he had taken the little *Sumter* through the Mississippi passes, he had become a world renowned figure. In the eleven months of the *Alabama's* life he had taken fifty-four prizes, burned forty-five of them, and sent the others on their way on ransom bond, filled with prisoners. He was received as a celebrity by the Boers at Saldanha Settlement and was wildly acclaimed at Cape Town. For two days he played hide-and-seek with the most persistent of his pursuers, the USS *Vanderbilt,* which had doggedly followed his trail from Jamaica to Brazil, and was now within a few miles of him off Cape Town. Eluding the huge *Vanderbilt,* the *Alabama* now set out across the Indian Ocean, a voyage of 4,400 miles which took five weeks.

Burning two prizes in Sunda Strait, the *Alabama* swept into the China Sea. While the pickings were slim, the mere fact that the *Alabama* was in these waters was enough to chase American merchant ships into port. Semmes steamed into Singapore and counted twenty-two U.S. ships lying idle and out of harm's way. This was reassurance to the Confederate sea raider that his trail of terror was succeeding in driving the American flag from the seas. With a brief rest in Singapore, Semmes turned the weary and limping *Alabama*'s bow once more to seaward, confiding in his journal that he would return to the Atlantic via Cape Town and perhaps Brazil.

New Year's Day, 1864, found the *Alabama* crossing the Bay of Bengal, and rounding the island of Ceylon. Hunting was poor, and once again Semmes noted that Yankee merchant ships lay idle, unable to find cargoes, and unwilling to risk a sortie into blue water as long as the *Alabama* was within a thousand miles. He proceeded on to the island of Johanna (Anjouan) near the Mozambique Channel, and after a short stop, headed once again for Cape Town. This time Captain Semmes did not go ashore, but remained on board for the three days it took to take on coal and provisions. He recorded in his diary that the *Alabama* was like a spent hunting dog, bone weary and sore of foot. He was anxious to find some harbor of refuge where he could clean off the long sea growth that now clung to his ship's sides, renew her copper bottom and generally overhaul the boilers, which were almost ruined from long and perpetual use.

Semmes wanted to try his luck in a European port for overhaul, and departed Cape Town on March 25 for a leisurely voyage north. Capturing the *Rockingham* en route he used the hulk for target practice before putting it to the torch. After two hours' practice, the executive officer of the *Alabama,* Lieutenant Kell, made a careful inspection. He found that many shells had failed to explode and that some had yielded only a low-order detonation, causing little damage. The defective ammunition, grown old in storage, was to play the ship false in her final action. Brooding over the future, Semmes sailed up the English Channel on June 11, 1864 and took the *Alabama* into Cherbourg, France, bringing to an end the most remarkable commerce raiding cruise in history.

FIGHT OFF CHERBOURG

Three days after the *Alabama* arrived in Cherbourg, the USS *Kearsarge*, a fine, modern steam sloop, steamed into the harbor, looked over the *Alabama* at close range, and took up a patrol outside. Aboard was an aquaintance of Semmes from the old days in the prewar U.S. Navy. John Ancrum Winslow, captain of the *Kearsarge*, was a capable seaman with dogged tenacity. Outspoken and gruff, he had been "banished" to European waters for some remarks he had made that Secretary Welles viewed as "semitreacherous." Here, out of harm's way, where his blunt tongue would not be noticed, he had patrolled the English Channel and adjacent waters in search of the *Alabama*. The *Kearsarge* had been at anchor off Flushing, Holland, when Winslow received a wire from the U.S. Consul at Cherbourg reporting the arrival of the *Alabama*. He quickly recalled his crew and steamed hurriedly to Cherbourg. In his previous history on patrol, Winslow had let both the CSS *Florida* and the CSS *Georgia* give him the slip. This time the stubborn and undistinguished Union commander wanted to be sure.

With his mortal enemy on patrol outside the harbor, Semmes pursued his aim to refit and clean his tired ship. Whether or not he knew it in advance is not recorded, but Semmes had chosen the one large French port which did not have suitable private docks for the *Alabama*. Cherbourg was a naval station, and the authorities would not allow a foreign ship to use their facilities until they received the blessing of the emperor. At this time Napoleon III was vacationing and would not return to Paris for a few days, so the French authorities courteously told Semmes that the *Alabama* could remain in the harbor until the emperor's return. Should this delay last very long, the *Alabama* would face interning until the war ended. Gradually Semmes realized that he was approaching an "intern or fight" situation which was growing in intensity.

In spite of the warning of his trusted executive officer, Semmes determined to fight his way into the clear, and issued a formal challenge to Captain Winslow for a duel as soon as he managed to coal his ship. The *Kearsarge* did not reply, nor did she leave her patrol. Accordingly, Semmes assumed that his challenge had been accepted, so he in turn prepared his ship for action and encouraged his men. Semmes' reasoning is clearly stated in his *Memoirs:*

> . . . THOUGH THE ENEMY WAS SUPERIOR TO ME, BOTH IN SIZE, STAUNCHNESS OF CONSTRUCTION, AND ARMAMENT, THEY WERE OF FORCE SO NEARLY EQUAL, THAT I CANNOT BE CHARGED WITH RASHNESS IN HAVING OFFERED BATTLE. THE "KEARSARGE" MOUNTED SEVEN GUNS: TWO 11-INCH DAHLGRENS, FOUR 32-POUNDERS, AND A RIFLED 28-POUNDER.

Later he claimed that Winslow had cheated, and that he had made the *Kearsarge* an ironclad without disclosing it to his opponent. Semmes likened this to a duelist wearing a coat of chain mail under his shirt. It seems a bit farfetched that this raider, who had used every trick and pretense for almost three years, who had flown the American flag to deceive his quarry, and who had lured the *Hatteras* to her death with false identification, should take offense at similar actions of another naval officer. Actually Winslow was only following the lead of the old master, Admiral Farragut, who had protected his ship's machinery spaces by layers of anchor chain, hung over the side; to make the arrangement more sightly and seaworthy, Winslow had covered the chain layers with smooth planking.

News of the coming duel spread like wildfire, and crowds flocked to line the shores off Cherbourg. On Sunday, June 19, Semmes allowed his men to finish their breakfasts, and at 9:30 got the *Alabama* underway for the last time. It was a beautiful day, with a light westerly breeze and a few scattered clouds. An hour later Winslow saw that his arch rival was making good his end of the bargain for a duel. He turned the *Kearsarge's* head away from land and steamed for about six miles in order to be well clear of the three-mile limit. Suddenly the *Kearsarge* wheeled about and headed for the *Alabama*.

The fight began at eleven o'clock with a broadside from the *Alabama* that whistled through the *Kearsarge's* rigging. The Confederate got off two more broadsides before her opponent turned to bring her guns to bear. The shooting was not good on either side, as evidenced by the fact that there were no casualties in the first fifteen minutes of the battle.

The ensuing battle was unique in naval history; Semmes sheered to port to avoid the onrushing *Kearsarge* and to keep from being rammed. Winslow then sheered to starboard, and with his superior speed attempted to gain a raking position by passing under the *Alabama's* stern. The slower *Alabama,* whose speed was reduced because of the amount of sea growth on her bottom, was then forced to circle her opponent in ever-decreasing circles. The pair of duelists completed seven full circles in a battle that lasted less than an hour and a half. At the beginning the ships were twelve hundred yards apart, but in the final phases of the fight only five hundred yards separated the two.

Semmes' gunners fired more rapidly than their Yankee opponents, but their first broadsides were aimed too high and were sporadic. On the other hand, Winslow's well-trained men were more precise, took their time, and made every salvo count. If Semmes had not been forced to close the range to avoid being raked, he would have preferred to keep the range open, because his rifled Blakeley guns outranged the *Kearsarge's* smoothbore eleven-inch pivot guns. He had hoped to stay outside their effective range and slowly pound his opponent to pieces, but was thwarted by the speed differential. Even so, the battle almost went in his favor. Watching through his telescope, Semmes saw one of the Blakeley's one-hundred-pound shells tear into the stern post of the *Kearsarge,* right near the rudder. If the shell had exploded, it would have crippled the Union ship and left her at the mercy of her slower adversary. Semmes counted off the seconds: one, two, three—what was wrong? The shell should have exploded. Too late he realized that the defective powder, aged and exposed to all extremes of climate in the twenty-two-month life of his ship, had failed him. The shell was a dud.

With this failure the doom of the *Alabama* was sealed. Slowly, the superior fire from the *Kearsarge* pounded the fragile Confederate cruiser to bits. "The firing became very hot," Semmes said, "and the enemy's shot soon began to tell upon our hull . . ." In contrast many of the *Alabama*'s shells would hit the iron-sheathed sides of the Union ship and fall harmlessly into the water. Seeing his shells hit without penetrating and explode without damage, Semmes shifted to solid shot. Again these round shot would strike the *Kearsarge* and bounce off. The exasperated Semmes sensed that the end was near. His men were slowly being decimated by the *Kearsarge*'s withering fire and his own batteries were ineffectual, even though they were accurate. His crew stood fast to their guns and fought valiantly, but convinced he was taking too much punishment and asking too much of his men, he turned the *Alabama*'s head toward the shore and set sail, hoping to beach his beloved ship rather than see her sink in the cold Atlantic.

Winslow anticipated this maneuver, and thanked his stars that he had originally steamed away from the shore, well beyond the three-mile limit, in order to have plenty of room to maneuver and fight. Speeding ahead, he crossed the *Alabama*'s bow in a good position to rake, and at the last minute saw that the Confederate had struck her colors. The Union ship held her fire, suspicious that the crafty Semmes was up to one of his famous ruses, and not quite sure what was happening, resumed fire for a few more broadsides. This action was called by Semmes as inhuman and contrary to all the laws of war, and he wrote in his report of the battle, "It is charitable to suppose that a ship of war of a Christian nation could not have done this intentionally."

Executive Officer Kell reported to his captain that the *Alabama* could stay afloat only ten more minutes. "Very well," replied Semmes, "send an officer to the *Kearsarge* and ask for boats to remove our wounded." However, the boats of both ships were so badly damaged by gunfire, that there were not enough to rescue the wounded, let alone the survivors.

Standing nearby was the yacht *Deerhound*, chartered by a wealthy Englishman named John Lancaster, who had brought his family out to see the fight. Lancaster took the yacht in close by *Kearsage*'s stern, where Captain Winslow called to him, "For God's sake, do what you can to save them." The *Deerhound* reached the bobbing swimmers twenty minutes after the *Alabama* had gone down, and started picking up survivors. They fished Semmes out, half drowned, and let him lie in the bottom of the yacht out of sight. When all the survivors were aboard either the *Deerhound* or the *Kearsarge*, and there was nothing more to do, the little yacht suddenly steamed over the horizon for England's shore. Outraged Northerners charged Lancaster with perfidy and collusion with the Confederacy, but the Englishman replied that "a drowning man in the open sea cannot be regarded at the time as an enemy to anybody, and is therefore entitled to the assistance of any passerby." Lancaster took his bedraggled guests to Southampton and turned them over to Confederate officials who hurried down from London.

Total casualties on the *Alabama* were estimated at about forty-three, of which nine were killed in action and twelve were believed to have drowned. Only one man was killed on the *Kearsarge*. Seventy men were picked up by the *Kearsarge* and made prisoners, but thirty-nine escaped on the *Deerhound* to England where Captain Semmes later paid them off in full.

The unexploded shell in the *Kearsarge*'s sternpost had a peculiar history. Winslow was reluctant to remove it lest he set it off, so it stayed in the sternpost until January 1865 when the *Kearsarge* repaired to the Boston Navy Yard. There the post was sawed off and shipped to Washington where Secretary Welles delivered it to President Lincoln as a souvenir of the famous engagement. Still intact, this little bit of history can still be seen in the Naval Academy Museum at Annapolis today.

In accordance with custom, a grateful Congress passed a resolution of thanks to Captain Winslow for his success, and promoted him to the grade of commodore. Secretary Welles, still somewhat chagrined that Winslow had allowed Semmes to escape, held up the appointment temporarily, but Winslow was such a popular hero that the Secretary thought it unwise to hold his grudge any longer. He delivered the commission with a fine letter of congratulations, thanking the *Kearsarge's* captain in the name of the Navy Department for the ability displayed in the contest.

Captain Raphael Semmes never sailed again in command of a Confederate man-of-war, but he did return to the Confederacy before the war ended. Lionized by sympathetic Englishmen, and even presented a sword by British naval officers to replace the one he had lost when the *Alabama* sank, he rapidly regained his health. After several months of recuperation, he made his way back by way of Havana and Mexico, not daring to risk the Union blockade off the Southern coasts. Traveling by circuitous routes, he arrived at Mobile for a reunion with his family, and then went on to Richmond. The Confederate Congress promoted him to the grade of rear admiral and honored him as best they could in the trying circumstances. He fought out the remainder of the war in and around Richmond, destroying the little flotilla when Richmond fell, and taking his navy brigade south to Danville. There he was accorded his last, but meaningless, honor. Jefferson Davis appointed him a brigadier general and still permitted him to retain his naval rank.

After the war Semmes was arrested and imprisoned in Washington, pending trial for his "war crimes." As the hysteria of the war gradually faded away, the desire for revenge likewise diminished, and Semmes was released in April 1866. In the sunset years of his life he lived in Mobile where he wrote his *Memoirs of Service Afloat*, which is one of the better accounts of the Civil War on the high seas.

THIRTEEN

Civil War Summary

WAR at sea made very few advances in the century and a half preceding the Civil War. For example, a seaman with John Paul Jones on the *Bonhomme Richard* could have filled a billet on Farragut's *Hartford* at New Orleans with just a few hours' brush-up drill—the eighty-three-year interval notwithstanding. However, as the Civil War progressed, there were numerous innovations and changes in both land and sea warfare. Occurring as it did when industrialization was changing the face of the world, the Civil War has been studied as the first "modern" conflict of the age. The more glamorous land campaigns, some of which were the bloodiest in our history, received first scholarly attention. For years after the war ended, descriptions of the land battles dominated Civil War literature. However, later study showed conclusively that the Union navy was an important (if not the deciding) factor which tipped the scales of victory for the North. Not even the staunchest advocate of sea power would claim that the navy could have won the Civil War alone. But it is clearly evident that the struggle would have lasted much longer if the Union had not employed its great naval superiority effectively. This would have led inevitably to either foreign intervention or stalemate ashore.

The ultimate achievement of the Union navy was the blockade of the Southern coastline. This is by far the best example of the use of this tactic in the history of naval warfare. As we have seen, it was a gigantic task which spread the navy over 3,500 miles of winding coast, dotted with inlets, rivers, and thriving seaports. The blockade taxed the North to the utmost, presenting logistic and morale problems that no one could foresee or anticipate. However, it proved its weight in gold and in blood, fastening a stranglehold on the Confederacy and denying that agricultural community access to the imports it needed so desperately. To a great extent the blockade dictated all naval action of the war—the efforts and strategy of the North were devoted to maintaining an effective blockade, while the South did all in its power to thwart it.

A lesser naval achievement, but almost equally important, was the capture of the South's principal seaports. The navy posed a threat of invasion over the entire Southern seacoast, pinning down thousands of troops that could have been put to better use in the Army of Northern Virginia, or in the Midwest. Coast defense became an important issue for the Confederacy, influencing some governors to withhold state troops to defend their shores in spite of Jefferson Davis' pleas for reinforcements.

As the great ports of the South fell one by one, the tasks of blockading decreased proportionally, freeing more Federal ships for direct support of military operations.

Naval operations of the war included the first real amphibious assaults in history. While navy support on the rivers of the interior at such places as Forts Henry and Donelson, Island No. 10, and Vicksburg gave the Union Army a tremendous advantage over the South, few of these actions were "amphibious" in the modern sense. However, the siege of Charleston, the capture of Mobile Bay and Fort Fisher, and even Port Royal are recognized as early examples of the kind of amphibious warfare that proved so successful in World War II. General Grant, like Washington before him, understood the advantage of mobile sea support, the power of great naval guns, and the devastating effect of an amphibious thrust. Throughout the war Grant used navy forces with more finesse and understanding than his opponents.

Few Civil War historians give adequate emphasis to the effect of river warfare. The navy's river operations were carried out on an unprecedented scale and introduced several new concepts. Tacticians of earlier wars confidently predicted that a well-fortified land emplacement could defeat and turn back a ship assault. This was considered to be standard doctrine at the beginning of the war, but it was dispelled as a myth under the hard-driving attacks of Farragut, Foote, and Porter. These leaders adapted well to new challenges, used their imagination, and had the guts to seek out and engage the enemy at every opportunity. Displaying raw courage as well as masterly preparation, they opened the Mississippi River and made it a Union stream. This projected the effects of the blockade to the South's interior, and denied it access to the productive fields of Texas and other Southwestern states.

The navy's great contribution to the war was one of isolating the South, and progressively squeezing the conflict into a smaller area. First, it cut off the Southland's foreign supplies. Afterward, naval victories at Hatteras, Port Royal, New Orleans, and Vicksburg persuaded England and France against intervention. The capture of the Mississippi River and its tributaries split the South in two, and allowed the Union to concentrate its larger armies against Lee in Virginia. Navy control of sea and river made it possible for Sherman to make his fiery march through the Deep South. Each of these accomplishments served to surround Lee with military force of increasing strength as the war dragged on. The navy's exercise of sea power was complete, and it permitted Union generals to move with a freedom of action that was never available to their Southern counterparts.

In calling the Civil War the first "modern" war of history, it is only necessary to point out that almost every art of naval warfare used in the eighty years following the Civil War was either already in operation or "born" in that conflict. The most notable exception is the airplane, but even with this exception it might be stated that balloons were used extensively for observation, frequently from barges.

The screw propeller was not solely an invention of the Civil War, but it proved so much superior to the paddle-wheel that all navies adopted it in future construction. Ericsson's revolving turret mounted on an armored barbette was immediately copied by the navies of the world. Although it has been vastly improved, it is basically unchanged today. Porter's mortar schooners were the forerunners of the LSMR's (amphibious rocketships) which spearheaded many an amphibious landing in the Pacific during World

War II. The crude Confederate mines that accounted for twenty-seven Union ships were improved and used extensively in both world wars, and in Korea. Cushing's daring use of a torpedo boat in a night attack against the ironclad *Albemarle* led to the development of a self-propelled torpedo and to construction of "torpedo destroyers"—which are now the fast-dashing small ships that are the workhorses of modern fleets.

The most significant naval developments of the Civil War were the ironclad and the submarine. The ultimate of the former was later exemplified by the mighty Japanese battleship *Yamato,* which at the end of World War II was the most modern and powerful ship ever built. Ironically, it was out of date when it was completed and succumbed to a series of aircraft attacks launched from an even newer state of the art—the aircraft carrier. The inventors of the Confederate submarine probably never dreamed that they were producing a craft that would almost sweep merchant shipping from the seas in later wars, nor would they have thought that a submerged submarine would some day fire long-range missiles with pinpoint accuracy. These achievements are commonplace today, yet in the early 1860's the idea of undersea craft was as novel and dangerous as space probes are in modern times.

Modern navies boast that they can stay at sea indefinitely because of their logistic arm and ability to replenish at sea. But the logistic problems of Gideon Welles' blockading ships, those weatherbeaten craft that stayed on station for months at a time, were equally great. Coal is harder to transfer than black oil, but these ships managed to do it, often at sea, or in a protected cove. These lonely watchdogs were able to rotate personnel, replenish provisions, and even take on supplies of ice at sea. Admittedly, they did not use modern methods but they did the job just the same.

Naval leaders of the Civil War were colorful giants of navy tradition whose deeds have been remembered by naming ships in their honor. Undoubtedly the greatest naval figure to emerge in the conflict was David Glasgow Farragut, who at the sunset of his career was the most daring and successful naval commander of the time. His bravery and defiance of odds have been emphasized in numerous accounts of his life, but he also set examples of leadership and forehandedness which are carefully studied today. Persistent, thorough, and painstaking in detail, he never left anything to chance when he could unearth the facts. He was realistic, as evidenced by his willingness to wait several months until he had an adequate force to storm the entrances to Mobile Bay. He took a chance in passing over the minefield there only because he had sent out small boat patrols under night cover to examine them. His patrols reported that many of the mines showed signs of deterioration from long exposure under water. He got his fleet past the chain obstructions at New Orleans by blasting holes through the barrier the night before he attacked.

His conferences with his captains on the eve of battle were examples of clear and concise planning, delegation of authority, and simplicity. He left no doubt as to his intentions and, having explained his plans, carried them out with a minimum of flourish, orders, or signals. So thoroughly did he place himself as the ideal naval leader that George Dewey, the "Hero of Manila," solved knotty problems in later years by mentally asking himself, "What would Farragut do?"

The most fascinating naval officer of the war was "Black Dave" Porter, a controversial and vain man who had fanatic followers and who made many enemies. Whatever his faults, Porter was a winner, unerringly following the philosophy of a more recent military great of our time that "in war there is no substitute for victory." He was overly ambitious, and wrote letters to friends in Washington that were so critical of his superiors that they bordered on mutiny. Yet he had a charming personality, was persuasive, and was a professional in naval warfare. Always willing to close with the enemy, courageous to the point of folly, Porter was idolized by his men and younger officers. He won the complete confidence of General Grant in the long and arduous Vicksburg campaign. Grant trusted him so well that he authorized a second assault on Fort Fisher after the first had failed miserably. His letter to Porter, advising him to "Hold on, I am sending more troops with a different general," set the scene for the final capture of that great fortification. Porter emerged from the war as the Union's best known admiral and lived to dominate the navy as the senior naval officer under the Grant administration.

Andrew Foote, one of the most promising naval officers whose career was cut short by an untimely death, set an enviable record in river warfare. A courageous, inspiring, and aggressive leader, he breathed life into his squadrons of little gunboats, and witnessed some of the hottest action of the war. At extremely close range, he would keep his ships in position and pound away doggedly at forts of superior armament, suffering an unbelievable number of hits and sustaining casualties that would have turned back a lesser man. Peculiarly, it was his fate to die from a small leg wound that refused to heal, rather than meeting his end in the height of battle, which was undoubtedly his fondest wish.

Many of the more junior officers performed well and creditably. There were Commander Walke of the *Carondelet,* Lieutenant Worden in the *Monitor,* and Captain John Rogers, who coolly examined the harbor obstructions under fire at Charleston. The navy still remembers Captain Craven, who stepped aside to let his pilot escape and went down with his ship at Mobile. Young Lieutenant Cushing set an example of courage when he took his experimental torpedo boat against the mighty ironclad *Albemarle* in a suicidal night attack. These and many more like them performed deeds that contributed to naval history, tradition, and to our national character.

History remembers fewer naval officers of the Confederacy, probably because they had little opportunity to distinguish themselves. At the top of the list there is Commodore Buchanan, who led the *Merrimac* against the whole Union blockading fleet at Hampton Roads, and who later challenged Farragut's entire force with the *Tennessee* at Mobile Bay. He was an experienced naval officer of the old school who was a popular figure in Washington in 1861 where he was serving as commandant of the Washington Navy Yard. He left the Union with regret, and did his best for the Confederacy in the face of overwhelming odds.

Raphael Semmes, captain of the *Sumter* and the *Alabama,* was popular in the South but was reviled and hated in the North. No one really loves a destroyer, and Semmes was probably one of the most efficient raiders and commerce destroyers in history. He cannot be classified as a great combat leader, but he did act courageously and fought a good fight off Cherbourg. He could have declined to fight the *Kearsarge,* a superior ship armed with protecting layers of chain, and was, in fact, advised by his superiors not to leave Cherbourg. Semmes, undoubtedly an excellent seaman, wise in the ways of ocean trade, was also a stern disciplinarian who molded a group of Liverpool toughs into an efficient crew that fought loyally at the *Alabama's* end.

John Maffitt, blockade-runner extraordinary and captain of the raider *Florida,* was an unusual man. In early 1861 he had command of the USS *Crusader* at Mobile when war fervor was sweeping that city. When a delegation of outraged Southerners threatened to board and capture his ship, he advised them quietly, "My vessel belongs to the United States. I'll shoot the first man that touches her." A few months later he resigned from the navy to join the Confederacy, but until that time he stood by the uniform and the flag that he had sworn to defend.

John Wilkinson, "Prince of the Blockade-Runners," was another of the "old Navy" who left to defend his state. The most successful of all blockade-runners, he was a man who believed in doing everything himself. He never took his clothes off when at sea, took his own chronometer readings, did his own piloting, and talked in whispers when making a blockade-run. He never allowed any unshielded lights, and walked about in slippers to cushion the sound of his footsteps. His last notable act was to lead a nearly successful expedition to free Confederate prisoners on Johnson Island in Lake Erie. At the last moment the plan collapsed through betrayal.

A great deal of credit for the Union navy's performance must go to testy old Gideon Welles, the Secretary of the Navy, who steered a safe and sober course throughout the four long years of war. He supervised one of the most rapid naval expansions of history and was never loath to sponsor and defend new inventions or novel ideas. At times he was severely criticized and ridiculed, but he held to the long-range plans of his strategy board and weathered the vicissitudes of wrathful public opinion. His fortunate choice of Gus

Fox as Assistant Secretary of the Navy provided him with an administrator *par excellence*, who was able to handle myriads of details and act as a front office man with officials on Capitol Hill. The two made an excellent team, despite their tendency to go overboard with their own conception of ironclad capabilities.

The Confederacy produced an amazing number of ships under the most trying circumstances. Many of these were converted river- or ferryboats, but some proved to be the most formidable ships of the day, and struck terror throughout an anxious Northern populace. Starting from scratch, the Confederate navy built or converted over one hundred ships; yet they did not build a single marine engine in the entire war. Hastily improvised shops and foundries devised ingenious ways to adapt engines from steamers, fishing boats, ferries —from literally anything that floated—into the hulls of their "warships." One of the greatest drawbacks of ships that were otherwise well designed was their mechanical imperfection. For example, invariably when the Union navy captured a Confederate ship, it had to be overhauled extensively before it was reliable enough for even routine operations.

Confederate Secretary of the Navy Stephen Mallory knew more about the sea and naval affairs than his counterpart, Gideon Welles, but he had very little to work with. He was soundly criticized for the South's being "so wretchedly ineffective on the water," but he retained the confidence of Jefferson Davis. The Confederate President expected little of his embryonic navy and consequently left all the details to his Secretary. Most of Mallory's technical innovations and strategies were sound, but he was unfortunate to live in a place where there were only meager industrial facilities, and to have directed a navy when industrial capacity was as important as naval know-how. He had at his disposal many well trained naval officers from the "old Navy" who were as able as their opponents and equally courageous, but they fought from a hopeless position of weakness. In Confederate eyes, the only bright spots of their naval history were provided by their commerce raiders and blockade-runners. Unfortunately for the South, these efforts proved inconsequential to the ultimate outcome of the war.

The story of naval operations in the Civil War is one of two vastly different naval powers. It is a tale of daring on both sides, but victory for only one. The South had no navy before the war, and no real capacity to develop one after the conflict began. Futility and frustration haunted a meager Confederate force, while success and honor fell to the Union navy. There were brave men on each side; men who did not flinch in bloody battles fought at point-blank range, and who could withstand the ennui and boredom of the great blockade.

In summary, the Union navy was able to play a decisive role in the Civil War, and sealed victory for the North. Indeed, the student of Civil War history must study this role well before he can fully understand that great conflict in all of its scope.

⚓

Aftermath

A⊤ the close of the Civil War the United States had the largest navy in the world. It was an expensive luxury for a young nation that was more interested in recovering from the war than in participating in international affairs. Feeling secure behind three thousand miles of ocean to the east, and an even larger expanse of water to the west, the country turned its surging vitality toward development of its great western territory and an industrial rebirth. Slowly the strength of the U.S. Navy ebbed away in an era of neglect and austere funding.

The blockade fleet was the first to go. Over four hundred ships were auctioned off or broken up for scrap within nine months after Lee's surrender at Appomattox. The ironclads were moored in the Navy "graveyards" and left to rot. In the haste of wartime building, the Union navy had permitted many shortcuts in the construction of ships. In some instances vessels became "ironclads" by the simple process of bolting iron plating to wooden hulls. The unseasoned wood forming the inner layer rotted swiftly, leaving an unsupported metallic shell, incapable of surviving the shock of gunfire, or even the mild turbulence of a fresh breeze at sea.

Suddenly the ironclads were gone, and the best ships remaining were those staunch old wooden ships of prewar vintage. Consequently, the Navy went back to sails and back to the old smoothbore gun. In 1867–68 when Admiral Farragut made a triumphal tour of European ports to show the flag and to be honored as the greatest naval leader of the Civil War, he traveled in the old wooden USS *Franklin*. European naval officers were amazed that the United States, the country that had pioneered so many new developments and had contributed so much to improved naval construction, would permit its senior admiral to go abroad in such an antiquated ship.

But in spite of the great cutback, naval authorities managed to hoard enough funds to finish building two seagoing monitors that were under construction when the war ended, and to complete the *Wampanoag* class of commerce raiders. The *Wampanoags* were the first ships to use superheated steam, but were shortchanged in berthing accommodations and coal bunkers in order to make room for larger boilers and engine spaces. As a result they were uncomfortable and shortlegged, but they were something new under the Navy sun. They developed the fantastic speed of seventeen knots and, like the sleek frigates of the War of 1812, were fast enough to run away from anything they did not want to fight. To postwar naval leaders, deeply impressed by the *Alabama*'s exploits, these ships were ideal. They were perfectly suited for employment as commerce raiders and were strong enough for single-ship engagements.

The new monitors made extended cruises to show the flag. The *Monadnock* went to join the Pacific Fleet by way of Cape Horn, visiting many prominent South American ports en route. Her sister ship the *Miantonomah* crossed the Atlantic in 1866 to call at European ports, and finished up her visit with stops in Russia. The voyages of these two ships were tributes to American know-how, and helped to turn the thinking of more advanced European navies toward the large dreadnought that was to become the backbone of sea forces by the end of the century.

Although the U.S. Navy was small, it was sufficiently experienced and strong to influence several issues of international import. The first centered around the French puppet rule in Mexico. In 1864, while the North was busily engaged in its war to preserve the Union, French forces had landed in Mexico and had established Maximilian as emperor. Shortly after Lee surrendered, General Grant sent fifty thousand troops under General Sheridan to the Mexican border, for the obvious purpose of invading that country and ousting Maximilian. Secretary of State Seward's wiser counseling prevailed, however, and the issue was settled diplomatically a year later. The United States delivered France a thinly veiled ultimatum which was backed in depth by an army and navy that was battle trained and ready. The French withdrew their forces, leaving the unfortunate Maximilian to face a firing squad. This was an overall diplomatic victory rather than a military success, and it was one in which Secretary of State Seward was able to deal from a position of strength.

In the ensuing years of the postwar period, the U.S. Navy continued to be extremely helpful abroad in showing the flag and in handling other isolated incidents of international importance. In this manner the Navy helped to protect American lives and property, and extended the sphere of American influence.

This form of "gunboat" diplomacy proved to be very effective on several occasions. Chief among these was the Rodgers punitive expedition to Korea. In 1871, Rear Admiral John Rodgers took ships of the Asiatic Fleet into the "forbidden" waters of Korea to investigate a report that the crew of the American merchant ship *General Sherman* had been executed when they were washed ashore after a shipwreck. In addition to the *General Sherman,* there were several other instances of shipwreck on Korean shores which ended in the mysterious disappearance of the crews. The U.S. Minister to China accompanied Admiral Rodgers in this venture, and carried with him credentials from the State Department which authorized him to execute a treaty of friendship with Korea.

Their greeting was anything but friendly. Shortly after the ships had anchored in the Salee River near Seoul, Korean forts fired on some of Rodgers' boats that were surveying the channel. Admiral Rodgers demanded an apology and for ten days waited in vain for an answer. Finally he sent a landing party of six hundred sailors and marines to destroy the offending forts. The Korean garrisons fought desperately with their outmoded weapons, but gave up the struggle after suffering many casualties. Rodgers was unable to renew negotiations in view of this warlike conduct, so he withdrew. The lesson, however, paved the way for more fruitful negotiations several years later. In 1882, Commodore Robert W. Shufeldt returned to the Salee River and signed a treaty with the representative of the Korean emperor which opened that country to trade with American ships and guaranteed safety for American seamen on Korean coasts.

[171]

Another well known incident handled with credit by captains of naval ships was the *Virginius* affair. This was caused by adventuresome American citizens who were overly sympathetic toward their Cuban neighbors. Cuban revolutionists were active against Spanish rule as early as 1873 when a so-called "filibustering" expedition of soldiers of fortune aboard the steamer *Virginius* was captured by the Spanish cruiser *Tornado*. Even though the *Virginius* was registered as an American ship, she was taken into custody and brought to the Cuban port of Santiago. There fifty-three of her passengers and crew were promptly executed. Indignant American officials ordered the Navy to mobilize and prepare for war, while the lives of the remaining *Virginius* passengers hung in the balance. Prompt independent action by Commander Cushing in the USS *Wyoming* saved the lives of the survivors. On his own initiative, and without orders, Cushing took his ship from Aspinwall (now Colón), Panama, directly to Santiago and made a vigorous protest. He was joined shortly afterwards by two more U.S. ships, the *Juniata* and the *Kansas*. The presence of this small unit calmed the stormy atmosphere and set the stage for diplomatic negotiations. Finally the remaining prisoners were released for passage back to New York in the *Juniata*, and the *Virginius* was returned. Although the Spaniards were able to prove that the *Virginius* was not properly registered as a United States ship, they did pay indemnity to the families of Americans who had been executed. It is generally conceded that prompt naval action, especially that by Commander Cushing, saved the lives of one hundred and two Americans whose execution might easily have led to war.

At scattered strategic locations around the world, U.S. naval officers who knew the value of advanced bases in naval warfare, initiated negotiations for exclusive harbor rights for American warships. In some instances their efforts were not ratified by an isolationist Congress back in Washington, but in almost each case the rights were obtained eventually. We have these energetic and farsighted officers to thank for our present bases in Hawaii, Guam, Midway, and for our rights in Samoa.

These far-flung operations caused some of our Navy ships to meet storms of tremendous violence. The first of these swept down on the *Monongahela* in 1867 while she was at anchor at the island of St. Croix. A huge tidal wave, born of a nearby earthquake, lifted the vessel far up into the business area of the city, where it sat momentarily, only to be lifted once again by a second tidal wave and deposited on a coral reef back near the harbor. Although five of her crew were lost in this experience, the ship sustained no serious damage, and was launched from her coral perch to sail the oceans for many more years.

In 1868 the gunboat *Wateree* was transiting from the Atlantic to the Pacific around Cape Horn. It was a pleasant journey with frequent stops for coal. On August 13, a tidal wave caught the *Wateree* in the port of Arica, Peru (now belongs to Chile). As is often the custom with these phenomena, the wave was preceded by a great rush of water from the harbor. This sudden loss of depth bounced the small gunboat on the muddy harbor bottom. From this precarious position her crew could look out to sea and watch a great green wall of water rushing down on them. The wave carried the ship well inland and left it high and dry at an elevation of about forty-seven feet. Only one man was lost. After the storm the crew had to fight off a group of hostile Indians bent on plunder, and having saved their ship from depredations by both man and Mother Nature, found to their dismay that it could not be launched again. In desperation the captain sold it to local businessmen who turned it into a hotel!

Probably the most famous of these storms occurred in Samoa in 1889. At that time, a scene of international tension between warships of England, Germany, and the United States was wiped out as if by magic. The hurricane wrecked three German ships and two American vessels, the *Trenton* and *Vandalia*. The HMS *Calliope* managed to fight her way to sea and survive while the others were forced to ride out the wild storm at anchor in Pago Pago. Aboard the *Trenton,* Naval Cadet Jackson distinguished himself by leading his men into the rigging to form a human sail, hoping that this act would steady the ship's head and relieve the strain on the anchor. While his effort was unsuccessful, he nevertheless added to naval lore and history of daring in the face of danger. As a parenthetical note, Cadet Jackson lived to reach the rank of admiral and in 1964 was the oldest and spryest living admiral, charming the residents of Coronado, California, with his vitality and wit at the ripe old age of ninety-eight.

Exploration of the Arctic captured world fancy in the last half of the nineteenth century, and the Navy participated with distinction in several explorational ventures. In 1871 the USS *Polaris* was crushed in the ice and sank, fortunately without loss of life. Eight years later the Navy Department assigned a volunteer crew to man the steamer *Jeannette,* which had been purchased by the American publisher James Bennett and donated to the government for use in finding a new route through the Bering Strait. The *Jeannette* was caught in the Arctic ice and drifted helplessly westward towards the Siberian coast until it, too, was crushed by polar ice and sank in 1881. The crew embarked in three small boats and attempted to reach land. After traveling for five hundred miles together, they were separated in a violent northerly gale; one boat disappeared and was never heard from again. Commander George W. De Long, skipper of the ill-fated ship, landed his boat on the Siberian coast; he and all but two of his men died from severe exposure and hardship. The two strongest men left the little camp and made their way to safety where they sent word to the leader of the third boat, Chief Engineer George Wallace Melville, that De Long and his crew needed help. Several months later Melville located the remains of De Long's group and brought their bodies back to the United States.

The indomitable Melville joined the Greely relief expedition in 1884. Commanded by Commander Winfield Scott Schley, three ships, the *Thetis, Bear,* and *Alert,* were fitted out by the Navy to rescue Lieutenant A. W. Greely of the U.S. Army, who had been exploring the Arctic wastes of Greenland. For two years in succession his relief ships had failed to get through, and his situation was extremely critical and perilous. Searching parties from the group finally located the remnants of Greely's party, a total of seven men, who had been marooned for three long years on the bleak island of

Ellesmere. This and other humanitarian gestures of the Navy appealed to the public and probably led to popular support for continued explorations. The most important of these, begun by Civil Engineer Robert E. Peary in 1886, laid the groundwork for eventual discovery of the North Pole shortly after the turn of the century.

The seeds for a rebirth of the U.S. Navy were sown in a small house on Coaster's Harbor Island in Newport, Rhode Island, under the able direction of one of the Navy's great educators, Rear Admiral Stephen B. Luce. In 1884 he persuaded a penurious Navy Department to authorize establishment of a Naval War College where promising naval officers could go for advanced study. After a shaky start in which the college's enemies tried to undermine it by cutting off funds, the first naval war college in history began to gather momentum. Luce brought to his faculty Captain Alfred T. Mahan, a naval scholar of some repute who had to his credit only one small publication on naval operations in the Gulf and inland waters during the Civil War.

Mahan took to the study of naval warfare with alacrity and, in the studious atmosphere of the college, developed his famous lectures on the influence of sea power in history. These lectures later appeared in periodical magazines and were later sold in book form. His first book, *The Influence of Sea Power Upon History 1660–1783,* published in 1890, covered the rise of British sea supremacy. It was received quietly in the United States, which was moribund in naval matters at the time, but it caught on like wildfire in Europe. His ensuing books brought more fame and honors from abroad, finally bringing his ideas to the attention of men in authoritative positions in the United States. The challenge of Mahan's analysis of sea power and his clear logic were instrumental in breaking the United States away from its policy of isolation to one of expansion. At the same time, Mahan's work created a spark of intellectual curiosity among a great many thoughtful naval officers who were themselves instrumental in shaping future development of naval organization and strategy.

Mahan's principal thesis was that sea power was more than mere naval strength. His studies showed that throughout history, true sea power depended on a number of other factors, including geographical location, physical conformation, extent of territory, population, the character of people, and the character of the government. In other words, a seafaring people, fortunately located in an insular position and blessed with fine harbors, could, if supported by an enlightened government, exploit the sea to its own great advantage. The example of England with her complete domination of sea communications, her profitable trade and colonial expansion, as well as her ability to defeat land powers less fortunately equipped, drove home his ideas to thoughtful men who had no previous interest in the sea. From his analysis of the fundamentals of sea power he turned to a study of tactics, and succeeded in changing American naval thought from single-ship commerce raiding to development of a fleet powerful enough to destroy the opposing fleet of a potential enemy.

So popular were his books in Germany that Kaiser Wilhelm II ordered copies placed in the wardroom of each ship of the German navy. In the light of historical reflection, it is also significant that more of his books were translated into Japanese than into any other language.

While Mahan was preaching sea power and larger navies with a network of overseas bases, another gentleman was quietly laying the groundwork for developing a new U.S. Navy. As early as 1881, Secretary of the Navy William H. Hunt established boards of naval officers and constructors to recommend a building program. The Navy had sunk to a new low, and had been overtaken by more advanced building programs of almost all the other major powers, and even some South American countries. The weapons of the Civil War, which represented great strides of progress, were now hopelessly outdated by progressive improvements. The newer ships were built of steel and were protected with hardened armor plate. Rifled guns loaded from the breech had long since replaced the old muzzle loading smooth bore cannon. Smaller rapid-fire guns had been developed, as well as new powders, torpedoes, and engineering plants.

The naval boards recommended immediate adoption of a building program to modernize the outdated antique ships of the 1880's. Curiously enough, the board recommended building a number of small wooden cruisers, which was heresy and Stone Age thinking according to a group of more progressive officers led by Engineer Benjamin Isherwood. This minority group recommended construction of armored cruisers and seagoing armored battleships. Finally the naval boards reached a compromise which led to the construction of the "ABCD's"—the *Atlanta, Boston, Chicago,* and *Dolphin.* The first three were called "protected cruisers," and were constructed of steel but were without significant protective armor. They did, however, have a thick steel deck to protect vital interior spaces, and were designed for either steam or sail propulsion. The *Dolphin* was a dispatch vessel, also of more modern design and with steam or sail capabilities.

After this breakthrough, the next decade saw a succession of legislative bills passed by Congress authorizing construction of various types of ships. It was hard for some of the Congressmen to depart from their isolationist views, and these misgivings often were voiced in the legislation by clauses which limited the design of new ships and restricted their operations to coastal defense.

In its wisdom the Congress later specified that all future naval construction, without exception, had to be built in the United States. This helped to rebuild our maritime yards and ship-construction capacity, which had fallen to new low depths in the hiatus following the Civil War. Modern warships required steel plate, gun forgings, engines, and shafting for which there were very few skills in the United States, but under the impetus of fat appropriations for a new fleet, American ingenuity produced these skills rapidly.

During the period from 1885 to 1889, Congress authorized a total of thirty new ships and encouraged the retirement of outmoded ships by the simple expedient of limiting the amount of money that could be spent in their repair. The Navy Department undertook a thorough investigation and shakedown of the shore establishment in readiness for new additions to the fleet, providing improved support, overhaul, and repair capabilities.

Gradually the venerable ships of antebellum days were laid to rest and the shift from wood to steel was completed. New ships, new thought, and young blood gave the declining United States Navy a shot in the arm which raised it from the depths of antiquity and inactivity to which it had sunk in its postwar apathy. As the nineteenth century drew to a close, a revitalized Navy was looking toward new horizons.

Index

⚓

Index

Ericsson, John, 61–62, 63, 109, 162
Essex (Union gunboat), 50, 51, 53, 96

F

Fairfax, Lieutenant Donald McNeil, 145
Fanny (Union tug), 37, 40
Farragut, Admiral David Glasgow, 5, 27, 32, 76–78, 79, 80, 81, 82, 86, 87, 90–91, 92, 93, 94, 95, 96–97, 100, 101, 102, 103, 105, 115, 118, 119, 120–22, 123, 124–25, 126, 127, 129, 160, 161–62, 163–64, 169
Fernando de Noronha Island, 152
Florida (Confederate gunboat), 32, 141, 147, 154
Florida Keys, 24, 139
Foote, Admiral Andrew H., 50, 51, 52–58, 86, 87, 88, 89, 96, 112, 162, 165
Fort Beauregard, 45, 46, 47
Fort Caswell, 128, 129
Fort Clark, 37, 38, 39, 40
Fort Donelson, 49, 51, 53, 54–58, 88, 97, 161
Fort Fisher, 33, 128, 129, 131, 132–33, 134–35, 161, 164
Fort Gaines, 119, 122, 126
Fort Hatteras, 36–41
Fort Henry, 49, 50, 51, 52–54, 55, 58, 86, 88, 97, 161
Fort Jackson, 75, 78, 79, 80, 81, 82, 85, 93, 120
Fort Johnson, 13
Fort McAllister, 108, 109
Fort Monroe, 21, 37, 43, 73, 132
Fort Morgan, 118, 119, 121, 122, 124, 125, 126
Fort Moultrie, 12, 14, 15, 17, 106, 109, 110, 112, 113
Fort Pickens, 14, 16, 119
Fort Pillow, 86, 89, 94, 97
Fort Powell, 119, 126
Fort Saint Philip, 75, 78, 79, 80, 81, 83, 93, 120
Fort Sumter, 5, 11–17, 18, 19, 22, 23, 31, 36, 42, 76, 106, 109, 110, 112, 113, 114
Fort Wagner, 112, 113, 114, 117
Fort Walker, 45, 46, 47
Fort Warren, 32
Foster, Captain John G., 12
Fox, Assistant Navy Secretary Gustavus, 6, 15, 16, 17, 53, 74, 75, 76, 91, 97, 106, 108, 109, 129, 166–67
France, 3, 144, 162

G

Gaines (Confederate steamer), 120, 124
Galena (Union gunboat), 121
Galveston, Texas, 24, 77, 151
General Sherman (U.S. merchant ship), 171
General Quitman (Confederate ram), 84
Genessee (Union screw steamer), 102
George Peabody (Union troop carrier), 37
Gillis, Captain John, 39
Gillmore, General Quincy A., 112, 113, 114
Giraffe. See Robert E. Lee.
Glasswell, Lieutenant, 114–15
Gloire (French ironclad), 61
Governor (Union side-wheeler), 44
Governor Moore (Confederate ram), 83
Granger, General Gordon, 126
Granger, Major General R. S., 122
Grant, General Ulysses S., 50, 51, 52, 53, 54, 55, 56–57, 74, 87, 101, 102, 103, 104–05, 128, 129, 131, 134, 161, 164
Greely, Lieutenant A. W., 174
Greene, Lieutenant Samuel Dana, 70, 71, 72
Gulf of Mexico, 77

H

Halleck, Major General Henry W., 50, 54, 58, 93
Hampton Roads, Virginia, 21, 26, 37, 41, 59, 61, 63, 64, 65, 68, 69, 73, 77, 132, 138, 145
Harriet Lane (Union armed steamer), 15, 38, 77, 78, 81, 85
Harrison, Lieutenant N. B., 81
Hartford (Union screw steamer), 80, 81, 82, 92, 102, 119, 120, 121, 122, 123, 124, 125, 160
Hartford *Times*, 6
Hatteras (Union warship), 151, 152, 155
Havana, 27, 30, 35, 118, 144, 159
Haynes' Bluff, 98, 99, 104
Haynsworth, George E., 14
Hiltonhead Island, 45

[181]